Owner's Manual
For The Human Mind

Alternative Title:
The Science Of Letting Go!

by **Doug Remington 2017** ©

ISBN-13:978-1981428342
ISBN-10:1981428348

First Edition

What it's about?

How to kill all emotional pain immediately! This is accomplished two ways. First it's done using the scientific process of sublimation, which is a term invented by Sigmund Freud but is exactly the same path taught by the Buddha, Aristotle, Shamkaya Philosophy, and many others. The process involves meditation and takes only a few days or weeks learn– NOT more than three months.

The main reason for sublimating all emotional pain immediately is to access and take advantage of more intelligent minds. Then by using mediation, we can take advantage of these minds, called subtle minds, for realizing our second and ultimate goal for killing all emotional pain immediately: that is, Ontology. Again we are talking about days or weeks to learn – NOT more than 3 months.

Although sublimation will kill all emotional pain immediately, it's more of a preliminary practice to Ontology. This involves the scientific process of – logic only – for determining what's real. The testimony of our senses is not reliable for making this determination. For example, the earth is round – not as it appears to our senses: that is, flat, etc. Only the logic and reason of science is a way to get beyond the illusions of every day life: that is, the illusions of every day suffering.

The word Ontology is most associated with the ancient Greek Philosophers. But it was much more advanced with the Indian Buddhist philosopher Nagarjuna. His book, Fundamental Principals of the Middle Way (First Century) describes the process. The book consists of twenty-seven (27) chapters of scientific logic and reason as to why our universe and everything in it is unreal, an illusion, like a dream.

Nightmares exists but they're not real. As soon as we realize our dream is not real, the emotional pain from the nightmare is gone immediately. In the same way, ontology proves with logic and reason that life and emotions are not real, just like a dream. They exist but they aren't real!

The Buddhist term for this is emptiness but emptiness doesn't mean something empty. It signifies something unreal. Nagarjuna called his system of scientific philosophy, Mahayana Buddhism.

The Greeks called it Pyrrhonism after the name of the Greek philosopher, Pyrrhon of Elis who developed a very similar concept. Tradition has it that Pyrrhon accompanied Alexander in the Fourth Century for the conquest of India. But instead of giving Nagarjuna and other Indian philosophers credit, he formulated Pyrrhonism which is basically the same as Nagarjuna's Ontology or Emptiness but from a different perspective: that is, what the Greek philosophers call skepticism.

There is a great book, Pyrrhonism, How the Ancient Greeks Reinvented Buddhism by Adrian Kuzminski 2008 which tells the complete story. There were earlier Greek writings based on Ontology. Aristotle's Physics depicts the physical world as metaphysical 500 BC– rather than actually physical. But Indian Hindu Ontological writings from the Vedas go back some 3,500 years or more.

Instead of Ontology, the Hindus named it the science of Brahman. Mary Baker Eddy who adapted Ontology to Christianity named it Christian Science. Even though various religions have Ontology as their core, the science of Psychology Ontology or, "Emptiness," as Nagarjuna called it, involves only secular, simple, scientific logic and reason. It contains no religious superstition at all.

**Therefore, anyone belonging to any
religion or even an atheist can
benefit from the science without
disrupting his or her personal beliefs.**

Thus the author of this book has decided to do commentaries on most of the Chapters of Fundamental Principals of the Middle Way, *Mūlamadhyamakakārikā* in Sanskrit. Emphasis will deal with ending all emotional pain immediately.

Mahayana Buddhism claims Nagarjuna's system of philosophy will eventually end all suffering permanently. That is, one becomes enlightened and suffering will not arise any more. But this is very difficult to achieve. It takes many years or even many lifetimes. The author of this book has not achieved this.

However, this commentary on the chapters of Fundamental Principals will deal only with logical reasoning on how to kill all emotional pain immediately – any time it arises. This of course is a preliminary to killing all suffering permanently. And the best part is, the process takes only a few days, weeks or months to learn – NOT more than a three (3) months. Needless to say, the author has achieved this, and so can anyone else who follows this same system developed thousands of years ago.

There are various stages or levels of enlightenment. Nagarjuna's book takes one to the Buddhist Fifth (5th) and final path, The Path Of No More Learning. The commentaries in this book will only take a person to the Second (2nd) Path. But this Second (2nd) Path Of Superior Seeing, and will kill all emotional pain immediately any time it arises.

No! A person does not have to
become a Buddhist to do this.
No! a person does not have
to become enlightened to do this.

A person form any religion or even an atheist can accomplish this learning without changing his or her personal beliefs about man, god or the universe. All the logic and reason for both sublimation and ontology are simply logical and scientific – not religious. The author has attempted to keep all religious views to a minimum.

Bibliography:
Buddhist

Fundamental Wisdom of the Middle way – translated by Jay L. Garfield.

Key To The Treasury of Shunyata – Sermey Khensur Lobsang Tharchin.

The Practice of Mahamudra – translated by Robert Clark – Edited by Ani K Trinlay Chodrom.

The Sun of Wisdom – Kehenpo Tsultrim Gyamtso teaching on Fundamental Wisdom of the Middle Way.

Nagarjuna's letter to a Friend – Translated by PADMAKARA Translation Group.

A Profound Mind by the Dalai Lama.

New Meditation Handbook by Geshe Kelsang Gyatso.

Journey To Uncertainty by Anyen Rimpoche.

Introduction to the Middle Way with commentaries by Jamgon Mipham translated by ADMAKARA Translation Group.

Nagarjuna's Seventy (70) Stanzas – Translation of text by Ven. Tenzin Dorjee and David Ross Komito.

Open Heart, Open Mind by Tsonknyi Rimpoche

Mother of the Buddhas, Meditations on the Prajna-Paramita Sutra by Lex Hixon

Perfect Wisdom, translated by Edward Conze

Deity Yoga by Dalai Lama and Jeffery Hopkins

Moon of Wisdom by Khenpo Tsultrin Gyamtso Rimpoche

Oral Instructions of Mahamudra by Geshe Kelsang Gyatso

The New Heart of Wisdom by Geshe Kelsang Gyatso

Masters of Mahamudra by Keith Dowman

Nagarjuna on the Six Perfections Translation by Bhikshu Dharmamitra

Mahamudra Tantra by Geshe Kelsang Gyatso

Universal Compassion by Geshe Kelsang Gyatso

Heart of Wisdom by Geshe Kelsang Gyatso

How to Control the Mind by Geshe Kelsang Gyatso

The Flight of Garuda translated by Keith Dowman
Garland of Mahamudra Practices by Khenchen Konchog
        Gyaltshen

Bibliography
Hindu
Panchikaranam of Sankaracarya published by Advaita Ashram
Avadhuta Gita of Dattatreya by Swami Ashokananda
Astavakara Samhita by Swami Nityaswarupananda
Sankaracarya's Aparoksanubhuti by Swami Vimuktananda
The Upanishads by Swami Nikhilananda
The Mundukya Upanisad by Swami Nikhilananda
The Gospel of Ramakrishna by M
Ramakrishna and His Disciples by Christopher Isherwood
The Teaching of Ramakrishna by Advaita Ashram
Talks with Ramana Maharshi by Ken Wilber
The Spiritual Teaching of Ramana Maharshi by Shambala
        Publications
Consolidated Works of Ramana Maharishi edited by Arthur
        Osborne
I Am That by Sri Nisargadatta
The Selfless Self, Talks With Shri Ramakant Maharaj edited by
        Ann Shaw
How To Know God by Swami Prabhavananda
Bhagavad Gita with annotation of Gudhartha Dipika translated by
        Swami Gambhirananda
Raja Yoga translated by Swami Vivekananda
Autobiography of a Yogi by Paramahansa Yogananda
Bhagavad Gita translation and commentaries by P. Yogananda
Bhagavad Gita translation and commentaries by A. C
        Bhaktivedanta Prabhupada
Samkhya-karika of Isvarakrsna translated by Suryanarayana Sastri

Bibliography
Logical Philosophy
The Power of Now by Eckhart Tolle
Stillness Speaks by Eckhart Tolle
A New Earth, Awakening to Your Life's Purpose by Eckhart Tolle

Bibliography:
Logical Greek Philosophy
Ethics by Aristotle

Aristotle's Ethics by Cliff Notes
Pyrrhonism, How The Ancient Greeks Reinvented Buddhism,
translation and commentaries by Adrian Kuzminski

Bibliography:
Christian Science
Science And Health With Key To the Scriptures by Mary Baker
Eddy.

Index

Understanding
Sublimation
Part 1

Do It Yourself!
Sublimate All Emotional Pain
Immediately!

Freud

Freud invented the word, SUBLIMATE! But he wrote practically nothing about it. Until now nobody has told us how to do it!

Now There's a Way!

Derived from the word, "Sublime," which means uplifted emotionally – especially in terms of dignity, honor and peace of mind, SUBLIMATE means: to change the mind from a negative PAINFUL emotion, like grief, depression, anger, fear, guilt, etc., to a sublime mental state including dignity, honor and peace of mind.

**Although Freud didn't believe in God at the time he
formulated the word sublimation,
he did believe in the practice of Virtue common to
all religions.
Sublimation is all about the spiritual practice of virtue,
but at the same time virtue doesn't depend on
a spiritual belief in god!**

In 1939 Freud did come to believe in God and said it's a good thing since it helped in his own case with introspection. Although Freud wrote virtually nothing about sublimation, he probably got the idea from Aristotle's Ethics, which was written abut 2,500 years ago. As we all know, Freud was obsessed with ancient Greek literature and even named his various complexes after names of characters in Greek Tragedies. For him the Greeks were highly skilled and advanced in their understanding of human psychology. Based on the following scientific psychology from Aristotle's Ethics, the reader will easily come to agree.

Aristotle's Ethics is based primarily on politics: that is, the duty of each individual toward the state. And so Aristotle's ethics is not taught for it's ability to kill all emotional pain immediately. Therefore, nobody actually practices the ethics. The pure brilliance of Aristotle's Ethics to kill all emotional pain immediately seems to have been lost.

Aristotle's teacher, Plato, was also obsessed with ethics and politics: that is, one's duty toward the sate. Plato's account of what happened to one of his teachers Socrates is still considered one of the world's greatest historic tragedies and is even taught today in high schools around the world.

Socrates is convicted on trumped up charges and left to suggest his own punishment which he does, but it's overruled by the court. Instead he's sentenced to death by drinking poisoned hemlock. A friend comes to prison and suggests an escape, but Socrates refuses. Instead he finally voluntarily drinks the poison after giving us all the reasons why he must ethically accept the court ruling – even if it's unjust.

Few if any of us would agree with Socrates and drink the poison. Instead most us, especially today, would have accepted his friend's help and escaped.

Freud comes to our rescue and renames parts of Aristotle's Ethics and calls it sublimation. If we were going to explain Aristotle's scientific psychology based on the way it was written, we would need four (4) columns.

1, Excess energy of the mind which we will call selfishness.
2, Balanced energy of the mind which we will call virtue.
3, Deficient energy of the mind which we will call self-
centeredness.
4, Politics: Our duty of ethical actions toward the state.

However, we shall do away with the 4th column: that is, our duty toward the state. Using the first three columns are all that's necessary for killing all emotional pain immediately.

Aristotle said,
"True happiness or authentic happiness lies in the middle of two (2) opposite extremes."

According to Aristotle, there are happinesses that come from getting what we want in terms of money, property, prestige, sex, etc. but these are not true or authentic happinesses. This is because those happinesses entirely depend upon our getting what we want: that is, money property, prestige, sex, etc. And when we don't get them, we are either not happy or down right miserable. This authentic happiness, however, exists all the time, and lies between two opposite extremes.

The extremes are selfishness which includes greed and anger. And self-centeredness which includes fear, depression, guilt, etc. Our minds react to the things that happen in our lives. When something good happens we are happy. When something bad happens we are unhappy. The unhappiness will either be from selfishness which causes jealously, greed, anger, etc., or it will be from self-centeredness which causes fear, depression, guilt, etc.

According to Aristotle, however, we can control our minds with the practice of virtue or *paramita* (Sanskrit). For example, love is an antidote for hate, bravery is an antidote for fear, and gratitude is an antidote for depression, etc. Once the emotional pain is sublimated, our mind is actually brought into a separate state of consciousness which Aristotle called the middle path of balanced energy. Thus we have the three separate states of consciousness in our normal waking state as follows:

1, A State of Too Much Energy
2, A state of Balanced Energy

The state of balanced energy is, therefore, the state of Authentic Happiness. Once sublimated, we experience dignity, honor and peace of mind instead of the negative painful emotion. Therefore, we can always be in the middle state of balanced energy of dignity, honor and peace of mind. This is done by controlling our mind with the practice of virtues in his book, Ethics.

Sublimation is not Suppression.
It's one of the scientific ways of
Letting Go!

Sublimation offers an alternative to willfully expressing our emotions like anger or suppressing them. It's a middle path. Instead the anger is sublimated (changed) into a state of balanced energy of dignity, honor and peace of mind.

If we examine anger logically, we find that it arises automatically and involuntarily. Depending our personal philosophy, most people will either suppress the anger or express it. Using our will-power to suppress the anger causes us to turn green and feel lower than whale shit. Or we express the anger and turn red, making a total fool of ourselves, screaming and yelling obscenities and perhaps even resorting to violence. Thus we vow to hate the person for all eternity.

Anger as well as all emotional pain
comes from what the Buddhists
call:
Self-Grasping-Ignorance!

How do we grasp? We know from Aristotle that our grasping is either selfish or Self-centered. But we should not accept this on blind faith. In order to agree or disagree with this premise, we must conduct our own investigation. Therefore, it's necessary to write out our emotions and examine them.

If we are angry, why are we angry? He or she did something they weren't supposed to and as a result we are hurt: that is, either emotionally or physically. If we are hurt emotionally, there is the old saying:

"Sticks and stones can break my bones,

but words will never hurt me."

Assuming we were insulted, yes it hurts! Why does it hurt? And why can't we let go. Forgiveness is an unselfish act. And if we are able to forgive the person rather than carry the ill-will and desire for revenge long into the night, our pain is gone. From this experiment alone we can conclude that anger is all selfishness and ill will. Again our conscious refusal to let go of the anger is again another clue, it's just pure selfishness.

More importantly, surprise comes when we decide to let go of the anger but we still can't do it. So anger is two (2) things. First anger is a conscious act of selfishness. And secondly, it's a sub-conscious act of selfishness. We discover right away that it's not an easy task to sublimate the mind (move it) from the path of too much energy to a state of balanced energy: that is, dignity, honor, and peace of mind. The practice of virtue takes great effort.

It's very hard to sublimate any emotional pain the very first time. However, once we accomplish this a single time or two, it's much easier from then forward. But in order for this to happen easily and spontaneously, it must be done daily. And with anger, its' also very painful, especially if it's done using love.

Meditation Comes to Our rescue!

We define meditation as simple concentration. It's no big deal. The concentration is as easy as sitting down and concentrating in order to solve a simple math problem. None of us like to do that. Yes, we need to use some will-power to make ourselves sit down and do it. Sit in a chair at a desk or slouch in a couch. Where we do it and how we do it, doesn't make too much difference: that is, as long as we actually do it.

Many of us have read books on meditation and all of that will apply too, but only if you want to use it. The important thing is to sit down close the eyes and concentrate. Many times, we are not able to forgive the person even during meditation. If not, why not? There's only one answer, selfishness. It's necessary to recognize this selfishness and admit to it. Otherwise, we will only justify the anger and rationalize its right-fullness. That is, he or she did this or that and we deserve to be angry. That's of course why we are angry and rightfully deserve to be angry – just like everyone else should be.

The Buddha comes to this exact same conclusion at the same time as Aristotle – 2500 years ago. The following is how the Buddha taught it. But it also applies to Aristotle's Ethics.

The Buddha Said, "There Are
Only Three Things that Cause Suffering
Greed, Anger and Ignorance."

Greed and anger are easily defined as selfishness. And ignorance is easily defined as self-centeredness.

While greed and anger are easy to identify as emotions involving selfishness, fear, depression, guilt, etc. are not so easily defined. Greed is grabbing onto money, property, prestige, sex etc. Anger happens when we are thwarted from getting these or someone takes them from us.

Fear, depression and guilt are all about me, me, me, and me. Depression says, look what happened to me. Poor me! Fear says, I need help to take care of me, etc. And guilt says, stupid me, look at stupid me – what stupid things I've done! Analyzed like this, we can see that self-centeredness deals mainly with fear, depression, guilt. All self-centered emotions are ignorance because they involve hopelessness and we give up. It's ignorance because this frame of mind is contrary to our own survival. We become couch potatoes and don't even try at life.

Five (5) Antidotes!
Scientific Ways for Letting Go!

The Buddhist Path Of The Bodhisattva
Five Antidotes That Will Kill
All Emotional Pain Immediately!

Buddha compiled the Sanskrit phrase Bodhisattva. It's composed of two Sanskrit words: "Bodhi," which means, "Intellect," relating to, "Supreme Knowledge." And Sattva which means the Middle Path in Indian Shamkhya Philosophy: that is, referring to one (1) of the three (3) gunas or constituents of material nature: that is, the Sattva Guna. This same concept is found in the Hindu14th chapter of the Bhagavad Gita.

The first verse reads (14: 1) "The Blessed Lord said: 'Again I shall declare to you this supreme wisdom, the best of all knowledge, knowing which all the Great Teachers have attained to supreme perfection (enlightenment)."

So not only will this teaching kill all emotional pain immediately, but at the same time it will lead everyone to supreme perfection: that is, enlightenment. Literally translated, the term Bodhisattva means many things. As the term applies to practicing the Virtuous aspect of Dharma (*6 Paramitas* – teaching of the Buddha), it means one who scientifically uses his or her intellect to keep their mind in the conventional middle path (Sattva) by practicing virtue.

Asvaghosa in his Buddhacharita (life of the Buddha) writes, "Buddha had Shamkhya 'pundits' or teachers, and so aspects of the Buddha's philosophy are Shamkhya." Sattva is a singular Sanskrit noun. That is, one gets into a single state of mind, Sattva. But this state of mundane mind has many attributes. It's also the same as Aristotle's Middle Path.

The Mind of Sattva
Unselfishness or Balanced Energy
Aristotle's
Authentic Happiness!

The mind of Sattva includes: dignity, honor and peace of mind. Additionally it includes love, joy, peace, forbearance, humor, humility, kindness, goodness, friendship, cooperation, understanding, faithfulness, gentleness, self-control, tolerance, gratitude, heroism, courage, compassion, etc. It's an altruistic state of mind. Compassion is it's highest view.

No emotional pain can exist in Sattva: that is, Greed, Anger, Fear, Depression, and Guilt will not arise. We're fooled into believing we need to develop these good qualities, but the truth is, we already have all these good qualities. We get them all as a single package when we are in the state of mind called Sattva. In fact we can not have any negative emotions or emotional pain while we are in the mind of Sattva or Aristotle's path of balanced energy which he called, "Authentic happiness."

In order to have these negative emotions that include all emotional pain, the mind must react out of the state of Sattva. The closest English Word that means something close to Sattva is when our mind goes into a genuine state of humility. According to Christians, humility is actually acquired from practicing Christian virtues, which are the same as Aristotle's Ethics or Buddha's virtues (*paramitas* in Sanskrit). No emotional pain can exist in a actual state of humility, and like Sattva, it's a totally balanced mind. Whereas our other minds are totally unbalanced with too much or too little physical energy. Sattva (unselfishness) is called the conventional Middle Path because it lies conventionally between two opposite, extreme states of mind: that is, *Rajas* (selfishness) (Sanskrit) and *Tamas* (self-centeredness)(Sanskrit).

All emotional pain is caused by selfishness and self-centeredness in the minds of *Rajas* and *Tamas*. This can be proven scientifically by experimenting in the laboratory of our own life. The reason the Five (5) Antidotes work for scientifically letting go is, because they force the mind into Sattva. No matter what form of mind training we practice, the following are the minds of *Rajas* and *Tamas* that must be scrutinized and severed: that is, scientifically killed.

What we call mind is really insistent hopping, skipping, and jumping about. But these are the same minds that experiences the gamut of negative human feelings, like greed, anger, fear depression, guilt, etc. And these are same minds of *Rajas* and *Tams* that must be recognized and severed in order to end suffering.

The states of *Rajas* and *Tamas* contain the conceptual pairs of duality. If something good happens, we are happy. But if anything bad happens, we become miserable. This is because of the imbalance of energy. Sattva is a balanced energy and consequently is not strongly reactive. Western psychology at least recognizes this state of mind and calls it proactive. So *Rajas* and *Tamas* are our reactive states of mind. Sattva is proactive: that is, it doesn't react strongly to the dualities of life.

There are only five (5) main categories of emotional pain. These are (1) anger, (2) greed, (3) fear, (4) depression and (5) Guilt. All other names for emotional pain are synonymous: that is, they mean about the same thing as the above five (5) emotions or are some combination of them. So Shamkaya Philosophy is very simple to understand. It's easy to apply also. This is because there is at least one antidote for each of the 5 categories of emotional pain.

1 Anger
(*Rajas*) – selfish category!
unbalanced by too much energy!

Anger always carries with it an element of ill will. Other names for anger are resentment, jealousy if ill will is involved, revenge, reprisal, annoyance, irritation, retribution, frustration, exasperation, rage, wrath, fury, bitterness, hatred, dislike, antipathy, offense, umbrage, self loathing, and many more. An immediate antidote for anger is: Affectionate Love. See Sublimation, Part 2 for the easiest and simplest way to kill anger.

When the mind is forced into Sattva, Anger, Jealousy and other hostility will not arise as long as Sattva prevails. When the mind is in Rajas, Fear, Depression and Guilt do not arise. Also FORGIVENESS is an antidote for anger. More will be added for dealing with anger in Sublimation, Part 2.

2 Greed
(Rajas) – Selfish category!
Unbalanced by too much energy!

Other names for greed: frustration that things don't go our way, or people don't do what we want, but lacking ill will: that is, jealousy, pride, desire, addiction, envy, lust, gluttony, excessive desire, craving, pride, arrogance, self-aggrandizement, covetousness, acquisitiveness, avarice, avariciousness, avidity, cupidity, stingy, tight wad, rapaciousness, rapacity, and more. An immediate antidote for greed is the virtue of renunciation and or the practice of Giving (1st of the 6 *paramitas,* Sanskrit, or virtues in English).

3 Fear
(Tamas) – Ignorance by way of self-centeredness!
Unbalanced with too little energy!
We become couch potatoes.

Other names for fear: dread, worry, horror, fright, anxiety, panic, alarm, anxiety, trepidation, apprehension, cowardice, uneasiness, turmoil, jumpiness, wariness, and many more. An immediate antidote for fear is the virtue of faith or heroic stance. The fear of *Tamas* is replaced with the courage of Sattva. When the mind is in *Tamas*, Greed and Anger will not arise. More on dealing with fear in Sublimation, Part 3.

4 Depression *(Tamas)*
Ignorance by way of self-centeredness!

Imbalance too little energy!
We become cough potatoes.

Other names for depression: grief, loneliness, despair, sadness, guilt, misery gloominess, melancholy, hopelessness, dejection, slump, hollow, self-pity, low self-esteem, self-loathing (can be either anger or depression), self-depreciation, humiliation, embarrassment, and more. Jealously also causes depression some times. An immediate antidote for most depression is the virtue of gratitude. One practice is to come up with 5 things each day for which we can be grateful. More will be explained about dealing with Depression in Sublimation, Part 3.

5 Guilt (*Tamas*)
Ignorance by way of self-centeredness!
Imbalanced too little energy!

We become couch potatoes. Other names for guilt: Self-incrimination, self-condemnation, and more. Guilt is actually a kind of depression. But it's separated because the formula for pacifying guilt is different than the formula for pacifying regular depression. An immediate antidote for guilt is the virtue of repentance. Repentance: making a firm resolve to change one's life around and never repeat the mistakes of the past replaces Guilt with the peace of Sattva. More about sublimating guilt in Sublimation. Part 3.

Buddhists (BodhiSattva Way Of Life – 9th Chapter) and the Hindu Brahma Sutra (2.1.1-3) refutes Shamkaya philosophy as far as Ultimate Reality is concerned. But the psychological facts concerning *Sattva, Rajas,* and *Tomas* can be verified in the laboratory of each persons life. No one can refute this science. The proof is, applying the antidotes kills emotional pain quickly. In any case Buddha coined the term Bodhisattva, which at the time had no other meaning: that is, using the intellect to keep the mind in the *Sattva* guna.

Buddha's statement, "Only greed, anger (selfishness) (*Rajas*), and Ignorance {fear, depression, and guilt (self-centeredness) (*Tamas*))} cause suffering." This is exact Buddha Dharma, Shamkaya philosophy and Aristotle's ethics. Or it's what the Western World calls sublimation by Dr. Sigmund Freud. In a way it's kind of a Rosetta Stone of scientific psychology from ancient times to the present.

More recently parts of Aristotle's ethics have been called Positive Psychology by Dr. Martin Seligtman, head of the Department of Psychology at the University of Pennsylvania. This is especially true using gratitude to end suffering.

Aristotle's Ethics is the same or similar to what Paul calls, "The Fruit of the Holy Spirit," (Galatians 5:22) in the New Testament. The, "Fruit," is a singular Greek noun with the following attributes: love, joy, peace, forbearance, kindness, goodness, faithfulness, gentleness, self-control. Even though Aristotle's middle path includes far more than those listed in Galatians 5:22, here is a clear evidence of Aristotle's influence. Early New Testament manuscripts were mostly written in Greek and so were the transcribers and scholars.

Although the mainstream of conventional therapists don't call emotional pain Self-Grasping-Ignorance, most all agree, it's necessary to let go of it. Otherwise it disrupts happiness and or peace of mind for long periods of time. Sublimation is one of the ways to scientifically let go. Ontology is, of course, the other method covered in this book.

Another way of dealing scientifically with anger according to Aristotle is the virtue of humor: that is, turn what made us angry into a joke. When I was in the army, I heard another soldier chant,
"Hurray for horses!
Hurray for ass!
Hurray for Captain Hardy!
He's a Horse's Ass!
Ha, Ha, Ha, Ha, Ha!"
For what ever reason I found this immensely funny. While I was in the army, and for years after I got discharged, I killed all anger with that little chant,
"Hurray for horses!
Hurray for ass!
Hurray for Captain Hardy!
He's a Horse's Ass!
Ha, Ha, Ha, Ha, Ha!"
I always felt good as soon as my mind shifted into Aristotle's middle path and the anger vanished immediately.

When I really got into trouble with anger, was when I stopped drinking and took up religion. I didn't think it proper to keep calling people and things a, "Horse's ass!" so I decided to live by the golden rule: that is, "Do unto others as you would have them do unto you." And since I would not like someone calling me a, "Horse's ass," I, therefore, agreed not call anyone else by that name.

Oddly enough, that's when I had trouble controlling my anger. In fact for the next 20 years until the early 1990's, when I found Buddha's practice of Meeta which will be explained in Sublimation, Part 2, anger was a serious destroyer of my serenity.

Naturally, I tried to use Aristotle's Sublimation of wishing love to get my mind into a sublime state of dignity, honor, and peace of mind. And this happened a few times but mostly it was too painful to wish love to my enemies and I couldn't do it at work.

Thus I became addicted to meditation, thinking long hours would eventually kill all my emotional pain – my anger. Yes, when I quite drinking all of my emotions were a mess. But anger was the worst. The Book Alcoholics Anonymous says, "Anger is the number one offender. It kills more alcoholics than anything else."

When I got angry, I definitely wanted to drink. And since I wanted to stop drinking all-together, I definitely wanted to do away with my anger. But this didn't happen with religion, or with the Alcoholics Anonymous (AA) program, or any of the other things I tried.

Then finally after about 20 years I bought a book of Buddhist Scriptures. In one of them the Buddha says, "Anger is easy to get rid of." This immediately made me so angry I threw the book in the trash and went to an AA meeting.

I abandoned the golden rule temporarily and I sang myself to sleep that night,

"Hurray for horses!
Hurray for ass!
Hurray for the Buddha!
He's a Horse's Ass!
Ha, Ha, Ha, Ha, Ha!"
Anger easy to get rid of!
He, Ha, Ha, Ha, Ha!

Then about 4:00 am I was forced out of bed by my resentment to see what stupid thing the Buddha actually said: that is, "How anger is easy to get rid of?" So I got up and fished the Buddhist scriptures out of the trash. What the Buddha said follows in Sublimation Part 2.

Owner's Manual For The Human Mind 19

Sublimation
Part 2

The Easy Way to Get Rid
of Anger!

The Buddha and Aristotle both lived about 2,500 years ago and promised a permanent end of all suffering by practicing a middle path. Buddha's first sermon at the Deer Park addressed what He called, The Four (4) Noble Truths of Suffering. The first (1st) dealt with the nature of suffering, the second (2nd) with the origin of suffering, the third (3rd) the cause of suffering, and (4th) the end of suffering. Don't bother trying to read this sermon to end your suffering. It's a waste of time. How to end suffering is hidden in just a few of the 84,000 sermons. The following is a single scripture that describes the easiest way to kill anger.

Antidote For Anger!
Meeta: Prayer of Loving Kindness
Killing the Fires of Anger Scientifically

Meeta is a Spiritual Practice that the author used to pacify his Bipolar Disorder, which involves a wide range of emotions: that is, going from suicidal to homicidal faster than the speed of light! Bipolar Disorder is NOT supposed to be curable. But that's only because mainstream therapy doesn't know about the practice of Meeta.

According to the Buddha, only three things cause misery: GREED, ANGER, and IGNORANCE. GREED and IGNORANCE are hard to cure, says the Buddha. But they are not serious faults. On the other hand Buddha says, "ANGER is a dangerous fault. But ANGER is easy to cure."

The Three Roots Of Action: "What gets rid of anger? The liberation of the mind by PRAYER OF LOVING KINDNESS should be the answer. In one who gives wise attention and practice to PRAYER OF LOVING KINDNESS, anger that has not yet arisen will not arise, and anger that has arisen will VANISH!" That is, anger can be sublimated by changing it into loving kindness.

From one's own personal experience, this is easy to prove. The Buddha says, "Monks, when PRAYER OF LOVING KINDNESS, leading to liberation of the mind, is practiced, developed, unrelentingly resorted to, used as one's vehicle, made the foundation of one's life, fully established, well-consolidated, and perfected, then these eleven (11) blessings can be expected: 1. One sleeps happily. 2. One wakes happily. 3. One does not suffer bad dreams. 4. One is dear to other human beings. 5. One is dear to nonhuman beings. 6. One is protected by the Buddha, the Dharma, the community of monks as well as the Meeta Gods. 7. One is not harmed by fire, poison, or weapons. 8. One concentrates one's mind quickly. 9. One has a serene face. 10. One is not perturbed at death. 11. One goes to a higher state after death."

"Monks, when PRAYER OF LOVING KINDNESS, leading to liberation of the mind, is practiced, developed, unrelentingly resorted to, used as one's vehicle, made the foundation of one's life, fully established, well-consolidated, and perfected, then these eleven (11) blessings may be expected."

(Anguttara Nakaya 11:16)

According to the Buddha, "One who is angry, automatically wishes the person with whom they are angry, seven (7) negative curses. The angry curse his or her enemy with: (1) physical ugliness, (2) Sickness, and All Kinds of Unhappiness, (3) Failure, (4) Poverty, (5) Bad Reputation, (6) No Friends, and (7) Damnation."

But says the Buddha, "Instead, these curses fall upon the unsuspecting angry person. By practicing Meeta, anger is cured, and the blessings fall upon all parties concerned."

Meeta Prayer:

"I wish (Name of Person: ___________ (1) Physical Beauty, (2) Love –Health – Happiness, (3) Success, (4) Wealth, (5) Fame, (6) Friendships, and (7) Enlightenment. May we be free from Hostility, free from Anger, free from Craving, free from Affliction and, free from Distress. May we live happily at peace with all beings. May all beings be happy!"

These blessings fall upon the angry person as well as all parties. Memorize the following prayer without the numbers:

Memorize the prayer. Or you can just read it. We don't have to mean the words at first. But once we've progressed, it's better to do the prayer as follows:

"I wish (Name of Person:) _________ Physical Beauty, Love, Health, Happiness, Success, Wealth, Fame, Friendships, and Enlightenment. May we be free from hostility, free from anger, free from craving, free from affliction and, free from distress. May we live happily at peace with all beings. May all beings be happy!"

As we repeat the prayer we visualize all of the Buddha's Love (or deity of choice – or highest ideal) in the center of our heart (center of the chest between the nipples). While we repeat the prayer, we visualize and actually see all of the Buddha's love combined with our own love as it moves up from the heart center inside us to the spiritual eye (point slightly above and between the two eyebrows) going out to the person we hate – transforming them into a person of loving kindness.

The spiritual eye is both the transmitter and receiver for the body. Therefore, when sending the love, the person actually gets it. As a fact from our own experience, we will discover that the person or persons, who also hates us, will lose that hate and in many cases become friends or apologize for their behavior toward us.

Or as an alternative practice, see Love expanding out from our heart center – going out from all four quarters: that is, above, below, to the sides, in front, and in back of us.

Recite the prayer for: 1, All beings. 2, All beings that breathe. 3, All devils, demons, divas, angels, dragons, cherubs, and other spiritual beings. 4, All females. 5, All males. 6, Your Spiritual Teacher. 7, All religious. 8, All worldly people. 9, All beings in a state of woe.

10, All persons you hate. Say the prayer over and over (a thousand times if necessary) until all anger VANISHES. At first, this is more painful than having a sword thrust straight through our heart. But when the anger VANIKSHES, LOVING KINDNESS prevails.

Loving kindness may not arise no matter how many times we say the Meeta prayer, but a feeling of dignity, honor and peace of mind will always arise. This is a fact from the author's own personal experience. Once we're used to doing this prayer of loving kindness, it's easy and pleasurable.

The goal of Meeta is to generate loving kindness. This happens when the mind is pushed from the anger of *Rajas* into the affectionate loving kindness of *Sattva* – the middle path.

"Free from craving" means to be free from the craving for love, prestige, money, sex, food, drugs, alcohol, nicotine, and so forth.

"Free from affliction" means free from disease, poverty, bad environment—all physical misery.

"Free from distress" means free from all mental misery."

The prayer covers all conditions necessary for happiness. It's a perfect prayer. The object of the practice of Meeta is to sublimate the mindset of anger into the middle path of Sattva: that is, into loving kindness.

Sublimate means to divert the expression or impulse of a NEGATIVE instinctual desire or mental reaction, like anger, from its unacceptable form, to one that is considered more socially, culturally, or morally acceptable. It's not suppression!

A feeling of dignity, honor and peace of mind is certainly more acceptable socially, culturally and morally. So even though a mindset of loving kindness is not achieved, a feeling of dignity, honor and peace of mind is certainly more acceptable than the anger will always be reached.

By repeating the Meeta prayer over and over, the very worst result is a feeling of dignity, honor, and, peace of mind. And naturally the anger will be gone. This will become a fact from our own experience by actually sublimating our anger. Also anger during that day will not arise as often, or as intensely.

I was a heavy alcohol user for over 20 years and finally when I quit drinking, my bipolar disorder kicked kin. I suffered with it. My sponsor in AA told me to stay away from psychiatric medications and I'm glad I did this. Then finally after 20 years I found Meeta which actually did control these wide swings of emotion – mostly anger. When I didn't practice, I was angry at every little thing, depressed, screwed up and crazy. When I practice the above routine twice each morning and evening, I was back to being a normal person.

This is the reason I was so regular with the practice for 10 years. It became a necessary sedative. Other than controlling my anger with Meeta, there seemed to be no permanent improvement. Then after about 10 years of practice, I had what is called a direct experience of emptiness (or Brahman) which killed 90% of the intellectual delusions that cause anger. And so I became like a normal person without the dire need to practice Meeta regularly. I still practice Meeta but its' not because of the dire need to deal with my anger.

Mahayana Buddhism stresses the practice of the 6 Paramitas. The first of which is giving. Giving love to all unconditionally doesn't seem like a very big thing. But without the practice of Meeta, I am not readily willing to do it. Also I find it helps with meditation when everything gets dry and boring. Also I still practice Meeta in order to keep my mind in the state of Sattva, which is in my humble opinion, the main practice of a Bodhisattva.

There is also a particular mindfulness practice that has helped me to pacify most all emotional outbursts of anger whenever anyone pushed my buttons. It comes from The Eight verses of Mind Training by Geshe Langri Tangpa.

It's verse 2 that it says, "Whenever I am in the company of others, I consider myself the lowest of all. And from the depths of my heart I consider all others as supreme."

In the beginning, it's suggested we memorize this verse and repeat it about 50,000 times a week – over and over! Otherwise I could not remember, and when anyone pushed my anger button, I just went bizzzzzark! Anyone with an anger problem knows how embarrassing this can be. That is, to continually make a fool of one's self time and time again.

It's especially embarrassing when it's your boss and you wind up getting fired. And it was extremely inconvenient when I told an Internal Revenue Agent what I thought of him. He stuck me with a huge unjust tax bill that took several appeal hearings to get it all wiped out.

This single verse, "Whenever I am in the company of others, I consider myself the lowest of all. And from the depths of my heart I consider all others as supreme," has been my savior from angry outbursts when anyone pushes my buttons. But it's actually the regular practice of Meeta that makes it work so well.

Second Method
How to Kill Anger Immediately!

In the author's opinion, killing all emotional pain immediately is contingent on our willingness to scientifically let go of our anger. It is the most intense and compelling of all emotions. It's also the single emotion we rationalize and justify as though it were our constitutional right: that is, our right to be angry – our right to revenge.

From this standpoint, it's necessary to give up all of our rights. That way we don't have defend these rights. And if we give up all of our rights, we no longer have the right be angry. All of our rationalization of what he or she did to us – that they deserve our anger is no longer valid. Why? Because we've given up all of our rights.

All of the justification of why we should hate this or that person for the rest of his or her life is no longer valid. Why? Because we've given up all of our rights.

Does this mean we can 't defend ourselves? No, we defend ourselves. And if we've been hurt by someone, if proper we go to the police or a lawyer, etc but not out of revenge. Otherwise we forget it. If we examine all anger, we find it's because our rights have been violated. Nothing more.

Once there is a willingness to Kill anger any time it arises, half the battle is won with all the other emotions. This can only happen if we stop rationalizing and justifying our right to be angry – our right to hate the person forever!

From this point forward there is a commitment to loving kindness! From this point forward we practice loving kindness in word, though, and deed, vowing to harm no one motivated by revenge.

Sublimation
Part 3

Sublimating Fear, Depression and Guilt!

Fear And Anxiety!
Anxiety Is Fear!

The Antidote for Fear (or anxiety) is Faith!

It says in the Christian Bible, "It's impossible to please God without Faith." (Hebrews 11:6) Based on logic and reason, it's also impossible to please any Deity or spiritual teachers without Faith. That's because most metaphysical teaching is based on faith. It's, therefore, necessary to actually accept some Truth on BLIND FAITH.

That's the only way it can be revealed. There is a Truth that not only kills fear, but also it kills a multitude of other ills as well. To understand it in the beginning, faith is totally necessary! This is the Truth, "Everything happens for the Good of those who take refuge in Buddha, Dharma and Shanga."

And not only the Buddha, but any Deity of choice, like God, Jesus, Krishna, the Great Spirit, Allah, etc.

The Practice begins by memorizing and then repeating the following mantra or verse, blocking out all doubt to the contrary. (It can be read off the page at first)

First Mantra:
Don't wander, don't wander!
Keep mindfulness on guard!
On the road of distraction

Mara (the evil one) roams in ambush!
Mara works on a mind full of greed and worldly lies!
So look into the essence of this magic:
You will know the Truth!
And the Truth will set you free!

This first mantra is helpful for concentrating the mind. The truth that sets us free comes by memorizing the second mantra and repeating it in BLIND FAITH whenever the pain of fear and or depression arise. This will kill all fear and depression immediately. If everything is happening for the good, how can fear arise? How can depression arise?

Examine all emotional pain. It always arises because of some specific bad that happens. Or emotional pain arises because of some good that was expected to happen but didn't happen. The Jewish Bible tells us in Genesis, that God never made anything bad. Whatever God made, He declared it, "Good!"

So if God didn't make bad: that is, He only made, "Good," how is it we experience bad and emotional pain? It's because bad is an illusion. Yes bad seems very real. What God did create is, "The tree of knowledge of good and evil."

Yes we have the knowledge of bad. But God declared everything, "Good!" Therefore, there is no actual bad – only the knowledge of it.

Second Mantra:

Everything happens for the Good
for those who take refuge in
Buddha, Dharma, and Shanga.
All situations are helping
me – not hurting me!

The above mantra should be changed according to belief. Christians might repeat:

"Everything happens for Good for
those who Love the Lord, etc (Romans 8:28)

All emotional pain happens because something bad has happened, etc. Bad is a conceptual fabrication of the mind – the dual opposite of Good. But ultimate reality is beyond both good and bad in what the Buddhists call, "Emptiness," or what the

Ancient Greeks called, "Ontology." And even thought this fact can't easily be explained, most all agree Emptiness is GOOD, since it means the permanent end of all suffering.

Everything Happens For the Good
Based on Ontology!

Ultimate Reality is a non conceptual GOOD. That is, it's a good without a bad which doesn't really make sense to us. But by taking refuge in the our Deity of choice, Buddha, etc, we take refuge in Ultimate Reality – this GOOD without a corresponding bad. The very first thing stressed in most all spiritual paths is taking refuge. And so we take refuge in our Deity of choice. Or the atheist takes refuge in ontological reason which will be explained later.

Why? Naturally it's because we think ultimately ALL GOOD will come from it. That is, eventually it means a permanent end to all our suffering. Depending on what this means personally, this could mean heaven, or it could mean enlightenment in Eastern Philosophy – something that happens while we are still living here on earth.

There are only two ways we can go. Either we are going toward this ALL GOOD – the permanent end of suffering – or we are going away from it. By taking refuge, we have faith and rely on our Deity of choice, the teaching itself, and our spiritual fellowship to lead us toward our goal. In this way we move toward the goal, not away from it. So good is happening even though the testimony of our senses tell us erroneously that a different bad is happening elsewhere.

We learn both ways: that is from the bad and from the good. But we learn much more and faster from the bad. So does that mean once we take refuge, more bad will happen to us? The answer is NO! Taking refuge is the beginning of the permanent end of all suffering. In order to encourage us, all suffering or bad is greatly eliminated with the preliminaries. Otherwise how else could anyone actually believe in a permanent end to all suffering? In fact once we take refuge, bad Karma that is happening in our life will diminish or cease altogether. Good Karma not destined to arise, will arise. So taking refuge is a win, win deal.

It works like this, by taking refuge in our deity of choice, teacher of choice, or the teaching itself, we eliminate most of the pain and suffering in our life. And the little bad that happens, will happen for our own good. When we go for treatment to a doctor, sometimes the treatment hurts. But we are usually never upset. Why? Because we know the pain is for our own good. That is, good is happening – not bad – even though the treatment hurts. So we are almost never angry with the doctor for hurting us.

Antidote for Fear: By taking refuge in our Deity of Choice, or teaching, we believe in BLIND FAITH – blocking out all contrary thoughts – that only GOOD will come to us in at least four (4) ways:

FIRST: we believe in blind faith by taking refuge, pleasurable good that wasn't destined to happen will happen. And bad that is happening now will wane or vanish altogether.

SECOND: we believe our Deity of choice, or teaching, will cause only pleasurable good to arise.

THIRD: we believe in blind faith that any bad that happens will happen for our own good – remolding, shaping and transforming our character and binding us more securely to the spiritual path.

And FOURTH: fear and depression actually draws the bad toward us, so it's imperative that we kill all fear etc. And for this reason fear is never a good thing. In the Bible, Job says, "Lo, the thing I feared has come upon me." (Job 3: 25) That is, when we are afraid, that fearful person, place or thing is drawn toward us.

Instead we take up a hero's stance, working hard by virtuous means to overcome and or avoid all bad – full of blind faith that only GOOD will come to us. And correspondingly by repeating the following mantra, and believing it in BLIND FAITH, only GOOD will actually be drawn toward us.

Mantra:
"Everything happens for the Good
for those who take refuge in Buddha,
The Teaching Of Buddha, And The Buddhist Fellowship.
All situations are helping me – not hurting me!"

Naturally the above mantra
should be changed to conform to
one's personal beliefs.
A Christian will do it differently!
An atheist will do it differently! Etc, etc, etc!

When Fear Arises, Repeating

The Mantra 50,000 Times A Day
Is Not Too Much!

But usually this is not necessary because the mind usually goes into the middle path long, long before then. It is also good to remember. Things which are pleasant are not always good for our ultimate good. Suppose we win a large sum of money in the lottery. This will certainly be pleasurable, but will it be for our ultimate good? If we spend the money on getting intoxicated, this may not be to our advantage.

So has the money done us good or bad? Things which are pleasurable may lead in the long run to great misery or *vice versa*. One old man told us, "My doctor told me, 'If I didn't quit drinking alcohol, I would either die of go insane within six months.'

"That was the worst day of my life," he said. "It meant I would have to give up drinking, the only thing that gave me any real pleasure. And so when I gave up drinking, it was terrible for years. But as it turned out in the long run, it was the very best thing that ever happened to me. That was almost 50 years ago."

It is advisable to repeat the mantra in meditation. Our gross material mind is not quick to grasp anything in BLIND FAITH. But in meditation, we access much subtler minds where BLIND FAITH happens more quickly and we actually feel protected. And so in meditation we can have this faith that kills all fear right away, but when we get back to the work-a-day-world, our Gross Material Mind will probably take over again, and our fear will be back.

Nevertheless we will easily learn how to kill all fear using this method. Using meditation again and again makes it easy. Our gross material mind will eventually remember, believing that only GOOD can happen – killing all fear of bad possibly happening. This happens as a sequence of logical thought because of our experience in meditation and actual life experience.

Basic Meditation for Ending Fear. We sit in a Comfortable chair, totally relaxed, thinking of our Deity of Choice, teacher of Choice, or the teaching. We adopt a hero's stance, repeating the mantra and envisioning that only good will happen. Naturally we also take all necessary action, like calling the police, not walking in dark places, etc. Fear arises mostly as a hopeless kind of impending doom! Once we've taken all the precaution we can to actually protect ourselves, there is nothing more we can do. We've done it all, what more can we do?

Although it seems utterly impossible, we come to believe

based on personal experience. Nobody believes it from the beginning. So pretending it will happen, meditation, and the mantra are a definite prerequisite in the beginning.

This same process will also work for depression. What causes depression? We can blame it all on something bad happening or something good that's supposed to happen but doesn't. Remember always the story of Jobe! The more we worry, the more the bad is drawn to us. So at all times, a heroic stance is necessary.

Another Way to Sublimate Depression! Using Gratitude!

In ancient Rome the Philosopher Cicero described Gratitude as the Mother of all Virtues. The practice of any virtue is a way of controlling the mind and keeping it in the middle path, Sattva, or humility where-in emotional pain can not arise at all. Many claim that gratitude alone will kill any and all emotional pain immediately. But in this writer's opinion, gratitude works best with depression and not as well with other things. That is, other things work better on greed, anger, fear, guilt, etc. But the KING of killers of depression is gratitude. Come up with 5 new things each day to be grateful and depression will be a thing of the past.

Depression is really just being ungrateful because of all the bad instead of concentrating on being grateful for all the good we have in our lives.

For example, you will find by experimenting in the laboratory of your own life, that it's impossible to be angry and grateful at the same time. It's impossible to be depressed and grateful at the same time, etc. However, I have found from personal experience which validates Shamkhya Psychology that Gratitude works better on the self-centered emotions than those emotions caused by selfishness. Gratitude does work on anger but Prayer of Loving Kindness works far better.

Gratitude is a prerequisite for the most important of all virtues, compassion. For example, we can be totally depressed ourselves and have no compassion for others with the same problem we have: that is, depression. Compassion happens when we have killed our depression and are grateful for the knowledge that kills our own depression. In which case, it is only natural for us to have compassion for others who have not discovered this secret for ending his or her depression yet.

Gratitude Works is a book by Robert A Emmons, Head of the Department of Psychology, University of California, Davis – 21 Day Program For Creating Emotional Prosperity. The above is a really good book. Used copies can be found cheaply on Amazon.Com and Ebay.Com. Also there is a great 71 minute, 59 second FREE video by Dr. Emmons called: Gratitude Works!: The Science and Practice of Saying Thanks on Youtube.Com.

Anyone who is depressed and hears that gratitude will kill depression or any other emotional pain immediately says, "I have nothing to be grateful for." This is remedied by searching our lives for something for which we can be grateful. In fact even those with depression which can be described as grave emotional and mental disorder can easily kill his or her emotional pain by searching and then finding five (5) new things in our life each day for which we can be grateful.

I remember telling my grandmother when I was about 10-years-old that I was depressed, that I had nothing for which to be grateful. My grandmother had a very sad life of poverty when she was growing up. She said, "I was depressed because I didn't have new shoes." Then she said, "I met a girl who had no feet." After my grandmother told me that story, I had no trouble finding things to be grateful.

I forgot all about the previous fact when I got older. Then when I quit drinking, the depression of my Bipolar Disorder kicked in, and I suffered with it for a very long time until I found gratitude as the antidote for depression again.

The Practice of Humility is Another way of killing depression: that is, we can take spiritual pride in being humble. This seems like a paradox but it isn't really. And we can be very grateful for out ability to be humble – a scientific method of letting go. That is, letting go of all our emotional pain – a method for killing all emotional suffering immediately. Once the mind-set of humility is established, we are in the middle path and no emotional pain can arise there.

Today I rarely have to practice gratitude because I do not usually feel depressed. However, I moved to Portland Oregon where it rains all winter long. For the first time in a long time, I found myself depressed because of the rainy weather.

Finally I found something to be grateful for and so the depression lifted immediately. I remembered how primitive it must have been for early Oregon settlers during the 1800's and even before. There were no cars with efficient heaters. I thought about how cold it must have been traveling in the covered wagons with no heat at all.

Also it's so easy to take a shower today: that is, turn on the hot water. How hard it must have been for the first settlers who didn't even have a steady supply of clean drinking water. I thought of all the dirt it must have caused inside the houses to have had to use fire wood for cooking and heating. I got very grateful very quickly.

Taking a Moral Inventory
Repentance:
The cure for Guilt!

It's highly improbable that anyone would read this book on the basis of having a problem with feeling guilty. This is because guilt only happens normally at certain times and usually the cure which is repentance, happens along with it. Repentance means to change around from a person who justifies negative un-virtuous actions to one who practices virtue.

Another reason this happens is because we are rarely able to admit we are wrong. We are always right, aren't we? If we have had a fight with anyone, we will always justify and rationalize who is at fault. And naturally we are never at fault. From the way we rationalize and justify the situation, everyone else is at fault – not us!

I once had a friend who told her mother she was involved in an accident. There she was sitting at a stop sign – minding her own business. Then this car in front of her suddenly backed into her car. So naturally she was NOT at fault.

But the investigating officer saw it differently and she lost her license. According to my friend, all the witnesses lied. And for years she maintained she was unjustly deprived of her driving privileges because of these lying witnesses who got her charged with reckless driving.

Then many years later she admitted to me, all that was nonsense. She was going too fast and couldn't stop, plowing into the back of the other car. Sometimes we make up excuses and actually come to believe our excuses are accurate descriptions of what happened – even though it didn't happen that way at all.

Sometimes it is very hard to admit the truth – admit we are wrong. When we are at fault, it's hard to admit we are wrong. Usually we rationalize and justify things in our favor. If we are going to end all emotional pain immediately, it's necessary to get honest with ourselves: that is, stop rationalizing and justifying things in our favor.

When we are Wrong!
We must promptly admit it!

In order to get to this point, we have to take what is called a moral inventory. "Moral," means the difference between right and wrong. If it is our moral inventory, it means, what do we think is right? And what do we think is wrong? It's not our mother's moral inventory, our father's moral inventory, our friend's, our wife's, or our preacher's moral inventory! It's ours. What do we think is right? And what do we think is wrong?

In order to take this moral inventory, it's necessary to sit down and write out the story of our life. We start with, "Once there was a little boy."

Or we start with, "Once there was a little girl."

Then we start looking for things we did wrong. Where did we harm others is what we are looking for? Selfishness and self-centeredness, that we think is the root of our problems. Where did we hurt others. The moral inventory does not include any rationalization or justification of why we actually hurt others. Only where did we hurt others?

We look for the first fight we ever had. We examine all the characters in our life: that is, first grade teacher, second grade teacher, all the students in our class, etc. We are not looking for people who hurt us. We are only looking for those we hurt. Naturally if someone hurt us, we automatically tried to hurt them back. We make a list of all the people we hurt back.

Before long we should develop a list of people we owe an apology. And because of our selfishness and self-centeredness, it should be easy to see that we hurt people far more than they hurt us. Is this hurting others right? Or is it wrong? It's for us to decide. No one can decide for us.

The writer of this book took such a moral inventory. Before I took this moral inventory, I thought I was the victim of fallacious harm done by others. But after the inventory, I saw that I had harmed far more people than hurt me. I stopped all the rationalization and justification. Based on my own moral beliefs, I came to realize that I was living my life backwards.

I was not really acting based on common sense and reason, I was actually a slave to my selfishness and self-centeredness. I wasn't living life morally, I was living life as a slave to my selfishness and self-centeredness. My whole life involved seeking pleasure and trying to avoid pain. And above it all, I thought I was a kind and loving person. Once I cut out all the rationalization and justification, I realized I was not a kind and loving person.

And because of what I saw, I wanted to change. My own moral character demanded that I be kind and loving. And the very fact that I wasn't, drove me with guilt.

I took this inventory as a part of the Alcoholics Anonymous (AA) program – the fourth (4th) step. Finally I tried to make amends by apologizing to everyone I had harmed – AA ninth (9th) step. There weren't many I could find other than my relatives. I wrote a few letters and called a few people.

And I made a sincere desire to change. I no longer wished to be angry. I began seeing anger as a defect of character. Finally 20 years later I found the Buddhist practice of Meeta, and this helped me achieve this goal – at least partially. I could at least kill the anger immediately upon it's arising. Also I no longer saw selfishness and self-centeredness as my friend. I saw it as an automatic, unwanted reaction – a defect of character!

On the plus side, selfishness and self-centeredness got me many things I wanted. But also it lost me a lot of friends and self-respect. Yes, it's instinctual – we are all selfish and self-centered from birth. We don't have to acquire it. No one needs to learn how to enjoy sex or a steak dinner. No one needs to learn how to be angry. The reason most people seek psychiatric help is to learn how to get revenge and be comfortable expressing their ill will: that is, telling others where to get off face to face. But this is living life backwards.

My moral inventory and those I talked to uncovered the real problem. Anger is the number one offender. It has killed more alcoholics than anything else. Most everyone who supports their ill will (anger) over a long period of time, usually end up getting drunk and not returning to AA. (My opinion only)

Based on my moral inventory, I no longer could justify and rationalize hurting anyone. This included animals. I became a vegetarian in October 1969. And at the time of this writing, I have been a vegetarian for about 48 years based on animal rights.

There is a wonderful story about Rabbi Hillel who lived in Jerusalem in the First Century. There was a wise guy going around to all the synagogues demanding of each rabbi, "Teach me Torah (the first five {5} books of the Old Testament) in one (1) minute while I stand on one foot."

Most of the rabbis got angry with his demand, since studying Torah is considered a lifetime work. One rabbi even chased the culprit up the street with a stick. But when the taunter got to Rabbi Hillel, he did not get angry. Instead he told the antagonist, "Stand on one foot!"

Then Rabbi Hillel said, "Make a list of all the ways you would like to be treated. Then treat everybody that way! Next make a list of all the ways you would NOT like to be treated. Then, don't treat anyone that way. That is the sum and substance of Torah – all else is commentary."

There is a Therevada Scripture where the Buddha is said to have given this same teaching in practically the same words. About 300 years before Rabbi Hillel, King Ashoka of India sent Buddhist missionaries to Qunram (a trading center) in the Sinai Desert. Many scholars believe this had a meaningful impact on the teaching of Jewish Rabbis that began about this time and the Jewish Talmud (writing of rabbis) involving moral issues.

Jesus summed it all up when he said, "Treat others as you wold have them treat you." (Luke 6:31)

No I would not like to be hurt by others under any circumstances. So I do not think it's right to hurt others under any circumstance. I would not like to be eaten by any animal. Therefore, I can not justify and rationalize my eating any animal at any time or under any circumstance.

All guilt can be pacified by understanding that we do the best we can with the tools we have. All guilt come from acts or omissions done in ignorance. By resolving again and again not to repeat these same acts, and understanding we will do better in the future, all guilt eventually disappears.

Acts of Repentance

There are acts of repentance too. That is, we can donate our time or money to some special cause in order to make up for the harm we have done. This is one way to relieve guilt.

Sometimes guilt lingers on. If so, we are dwelling in ignorance. Dwelling in this kind of ignorance draws negativity to us. So not only does guilt cause unwanted suffering, it draws unwanted bad karma too. Therefore, it's best to kill all guilt any time it arises.

By treating others as we would also like to be treated will keep our mind in the middle path of Buddha and Aristotle. Additionally this can work as an act of repentance.

Another act of repentance involves confession. It's possible to go to any Catholic Church, contact any priest – even though we're not Catholic – and confess all the wrongs we have committed. The priest is bound by an Oath to the Catholic Church to keep all of our secrets.

Even the courts can not compel the priest to divulge any of our secrets. It's called penitent privilege. And so we can trust a Catholic priest to keep the secrets of the confession as a repentant act. Attorneys also have this same privilege but it's called client privilege.

This is important if we have committed any illegal acts. Confessing to our psychiatrist is not a good idea, because he or she is not bound to keep our secrets and can be compelled in court to divulge anything we tell or don't tell them. Not all clergy are bound by penitent privilege. So if we are going to confess anything we want kept secret, it's better to ask our clergy if they are bound by penitent privilege before confessing.

Acts of repentance can be the very best way to kill all guilt immediately. But ultimately guilt returns again and again like all the emotions. Based on this approach, over time eventually the author's guilt dwindled away.

Sublimation
Part 4
Karma Yoga
The Answer To The Secret Of Life!
How to End All Problems!

Santadevi tells us, "All problems and unhappiness come from seeking pleasure and trying to avoid pain. That is, we instinctively seek happiness by a means that is the very cause of our unhappiness." How can this be?

From the beginning of our life, we instinctively sought happiness as a main motivation. It's this very motivation that causes all the trouble. It's only natural that we seek happiness by enjoying money, property, prestige, sex, etc. If we obtain these pleasures, we are happy. But if we investigate, we find, it's our old enemy selfishness and self-centeredness. This enemy tells us, "I want what I want, when I want it!"

But life deals out, whatever we get – if we ever get it. And when we don't get what we want, we are either greedy, angry, fearful, depressed or guilty. Is there a better way?

Yes there is. Our motivation: that is, working for ourselves, is total stupidity! When life denies us the things we want, it will always cause some degree of misery. It's like someone going to the doctor and asking, "How do I end my headaches?

And the doctor answers, "By not hitting yourself over the head with that hammer."

In fact working for ourselves is exactly like someone hitting themselves over the head. In fact, that's exactly what we do. We hit ourselves over the head with our hammer, selfishness and self-centeredness every time life refuses any of our demands. But is there another way?

Yes, there's a better way! We simply stop working for ourselves. There are at least two more intelligent ways to work.

The first way does not involve a belief in God. And the second way does. We will examine the first way first. No belief in God is necessary.

We will change our motive in life. From now on, we will stop working for ourselves. Instead of trying to make ourselves happy with our every action, we will strive to make others happy. Our motive in life changes.

Our selfishness and self-centeredness dictates that we pack as little into life as possible, and we take from life as much as we can. Instead – from now on – we will pack as much into the stream of life as possible: that is, trying to make others happy. And we will take nothing or as little as possible for ourselves. If by accident, however, we do get some happiness out of life, that's okay too.

Our duty in life becomes: to make others happy! Most of us need a job to obtain the necessities of life or perhaps we are in business for ourselves. It doesn't matter. Our newly found motive in life is to make others happy. If we have a job, our first duty is to our boss – our employer: that is, to make him or her happy – not ourselves. We do this by voluntarily working above and beyond what is required to keep the job. That is the very best way to make our boss happy. We come to work on time and contribute a full day's work.

Or if we are in business for ourselves, our first duty is to our customers and our employees. We realine our thinking to serving others – not ourselves.

But what if we try very hard, and we still can not make others happy – no matter how hard we try? As we will learn from the facts from of our own experience, we shall discover a very important truth. If we don't make others happy, we shall not normally be very upset. Why? That's because we are not normally selfishly and self-centeredly attached to making others happy. We are only normally selfishly and self-centeredly attached to making ourselves happy.

So when we don't make others happy – no matter how hard we try – this will not cause a problem.

Later in this book we shall show ontologically, with logic and reason, that this self we treasure so greatly and we try to please constantly, doesn't really exist. It is actually an illusion, unreal, like the self in our dreams.

The big problem of course is when we do make others happy. We can feel very good about doing this and in time, we may get super attached to this aspect. In this case, if we then don't make others happy, we could possibly suffer shame or remorse. Instead we offer the credit for success or failure of our effort to our highest ideal and duty: that is, for example, to the well-being of all humanity. Or in the case of Aristotle's Ethics, we work for the betterment of the state. That is, the society would be much better off and stronger if all it's members worked with this kind of a motive.

If the results are good, and we do actually make others happy, it belongs to our highest ideal and duty – not to ourselves. Our self doesn't really exist as we shall find out later. If the results are bad, and nobody is happy, instead of heaping this failure on ourselves, we dedicate it to our highest ideals. And we do the same thing when the results are good. That is, we get out of the results business. We stay constantly in the footwork business of trying to make others happy. The pain and suffering of life is not in the footwork as much as in the results.

By dedicating the results (getting out of the results – good or bad) we eliminate all possibility of things not going our way. That is, by dedicating the, "Fruits of actions." as it's called in the Hindu scripture, the Bhagavad Gita, we can be happy all the time. That's because dedicating the results of actions (good or bad) forces the mind into the sublime middle path of Aristotle, Buddha, the Shamkayas and Freud.

Therefore, we can be in a mental state of dignity, honor and peace of mind all the time. This is true if things do not go our way. And this will happen if things do go our way – which is never a problem.

Naturally this doesn't happen without being able to control our mind. And it doesn't happen easily. Even though we try to do work for the happiness of others, our selfishness and self-centeredness will constantly put up a fight. And so it takes great effort to dedicate the fruits of actions to our ideal. But finally we squeeze out all selfishness and self-centeredness. And when this happens, our mind eases into a space-like vacuity and all emotional suffering will be gone immediately.

This is the same space-like vacuity the mind goes into with the practice of emptiness or ontology which will be discussed later, in the chapters that follow. Using Karma Yoga, the mind goes into the space-like vacuity as a result of letting go of the results of our actions – letting go of good and bad. Using sublimation, is a scientific way of letting go of our misery. Ontology is an even better way.

The twenty-seven (27) chapters of Fundamental Principals offer a way of scientifically letting go using ontology. Consequently they are the same practice as karma Yoga but from different standpoints. We verify this as a result of personal experience. In both cases our mind finally eases into a space-like vacuity that kills all emotional pain. What remains is infallible peace.

The second method of practicing Karma Yoga involves dedicating the fruits of actions to God.

How the Author of this Book
Practiced Karma Yoga
Using a Belief In God:

I tried practicing Karma Yoga with different gods: that is, Krishna, Jesus, Allah, the Holy Spirit, the Christian and Jewish God, etc. for years. Finally, I settled upon Buddha. Basically Karma Yoga works the same with any or even all the Gods.

The Buddha is NOT considered a God by Buddhists. But this is not true of the Hindus. They believe only God can found a new religion, as Buddha did. Firstly and foremostly this is because, if Buddha would have been an ordinary person, he could not have attracted so many followers over the past 2500 years.

In the Mahayana Buddhist path the Sanskrit words *Bhagavan* which means, He, who is worthy of worship, and *Bhagavani* which means, She who is worthy of worship, have existed from antiquity. In this tradition, all Buddhas, male and female are placed on the same level of worship just like Gods. But they are not considered to be Gods themselves.

There are major problems in life, like earning a living and love relationships. If these problems are not solved, they gnaw at our serenity and drive us crazy with problems. Problems are defined as obstructions to our happiness that lack a viable plan. As long there is a viable plan, there is no problem. If we need money and have a viable plan to get it, where's the problem? This fact must be verified by experimenting in the laboratory of our own lives.

As long as we have a viable plan to solve any problem, there is really no problem. We know what we're going to do to overcome. But when one or more problems drag on for years and years, we lose hope. And really this is how most of us find the spiritual path. We find meditation, for example, and from the very beginning, we find some peace and happiness – very slight at first. Our problems are gone. But they're only gone temporarily in meditation. The problems of love relationships and money may drag on year after year when we're not in meditation.

Once we're back to the work-a-day-world of hustle and bustle, our problems come back – still gnawing at us in the backs of our minds. There is a simple way to solve all these major and minor problems but most people don't know how to do it.

It's Called Karma Yoga!

No! Karma Yoga has nothing to do with the physical exercises. Some Yoga does involve physical exercises. It's called Hatha Yoga which was designed thousands of years ago to keep the body healthy. Instead Karma Yoga, which involves no physical exercises, was designed thousands of years ago to keep our minds healthy.

What Is Karma Yoga? It Involves Three (3) Things: 1, Taking Refuge in Our Deity of Choice! (God, Buddha, Krishna, etc.) 2, Going to Work for our Deity of choice! 3, Dedicating the Fruits of Actions (results of actions) to our Deity of choice.

One (1), We take Refuge In Our Deity of Choice! (Buddha, God, etc.) This is done by memorizing the following prayer and repeating it many times every day.

"God, Buddha, etc, I offer myself to you – to build with me and to do with me as you will. Relieve me of the bondage of self, that I may better do your will. Take away my difficulties that victory over them may bare witness of your power, love and way of life. May I do your will always."

By repeating this prayer many times a day, we take it on blind faith that only Good and happiness will come to us. From this point onward, it's no longer our responsibility to be happy. It's now our Deity's responsibility to provide happiness for us.

Two (2), We go to Work for Deity! All emotional pain comes from selfishness and self-centeredness – working for ourselves. Instead we go to work for our Deity of Choice – not ourselves. This becomes a seven (7) day a week job, 365 days a year, and 24 hours a day. We never take a vacation because we never need a vacation. That's because the practice of Karma Yoga is totally refreshing.

Now comes the hard part. We only use the following prayer

– never paying for specific solutions to problems. This is the important part of Karma Yoga: that is, we pray only,
"Lord Buddha (or Deity of choice, etc.), please give us the knowledge of your will for me and the power to carry that out."

The Christian Bible says, "And when you pray, do not be like the pagans, for they think their many words will be heard. Do not be like them, for your Father (God, Buddha, etc.) knows what you need before you ask." (Matthew 6: 7-8)

If Deity already knows what you need, then why ask specifically? But it is permissible to pray for others. All the pain and suffering of life comes from being selfishly an self-centeredly attached to the results of our own life. By praying selfishly and selfcenteredly for specific things, God, Buddha, etc. (by default) becomes our servant. Therefore, since we are working for Deity, and we are their servant, we pray only for their knowledge of how we should serve: that is, what we should do.

Otherwise we fall into a degenerate position of being attached to and seeking only the pleasures of life. That is, "Give us money, property, prestige and sex." And when we don't get these things, we're miserable. Instead the Karma Yogi takes up his or her constitutional position as SERVANT, praying only for the knowledge of Deity's will and the power for us to carry that out.

Instead of trying to please ourselves, we have only one job in life: that is, to please our Deity of choice and engage in the welfare of all beings: that is, make others happy. How? What we normally do for ourselves, we do that exact same thing. But now we do it as Deity's personal servant. Then it becomes our, "Duty," to make our Deity and our fellow beings directly happy.

Any happiness for ourselves comes indirectly. All the pain and suffering in life comes from trying to make ourselves happy: that is, working for ourselves. This problem is solved by Karma Yoga. If our job is road construction, filling the pot holes in the streets, we work as our Deity's personal servant, fixing the streets and making drivers happy!

Three (3), We dedicate the Fruits of Actions (results of actions) to Deity! It's the secret to detachment! It's the secret of scientifically letting go. This too is a hard part. We have to be willing to dedicate the results of all our actions to our Deity – especially the good, the bad. That is, we don't take personal credit for any of our actions. And we don't take the blame for them either. Whatever happens, happens! We let the chips fall where they may.

But this is only common sense and reason. We really don't

have a choice. This sounds like we become indifferent to life. That is, we don't really care. NO! We care! We make an effort to please God and those around us. And we work hard to win. Hard work and caring are the core of Karma Yoga. We do care that the work be successful. We work hard for success. But we dedicate the results – never taking personal credit or blame for our action. "Man proposes but God disposes." (Proverbs 19: 21)

Dedicating the fruits of our actions (Karma Yoga) makes detachment a thousand times easier. If we make a million dollars, that belongs to our Deity of Choice. If we go broke and end-up starving to death on the streets, that also belongs to our Deity of Choice – not to us. We take no credit or blame. Because it puts our minds in the middle path, we automatically have a feeling of dignity, honor and peace of mind.

Karma Yoga Kills All Problems!

My Christian friends tell me, everyone has problems – even Jesus had problems. But my Christian friends don't practice Karma Yoga. So they don't know this is possible. The Karma Yogi establishes him or herself in their constitutional position of being the servant of the Lord. This constitutional position is the opposite of selfishness and self-centeredness. The Karma Yogi's constitutional duty is simple: he or she has the duty of serving the Lord and making others happy – not trying to make him or herself happy.

This is the opposite duty of a person who acts instinctively, seeking the pleasures of money, property, prestige, sex, etc. Any person who thinks he or she has the duty and obligation to be successful at achieving the pleasures of life is a person full of problems galore. This is because whatever we own will give us problems.

If we own goats, we will have goat problems. If we have money, we will have money problems. If we have children, we have child problems. But we can get rid of all these problems by dedicating the results of life: that is, if we win or lose is dedicated to our deity of Choice. We give up our instinctual duty we were born with to a more scientific duty – one that can always be achieved.

We can always do our duty. We can always take action to make others happy. And even if we can't actually take physical action to help, we can always maintain this duty mentally. Man proposes but God disposes. So no matter how the results of life turn out, we can always do our duty. And we most always know what our duty is. Once this constitutional position of serving our Deity of Choice is accepted as a duty all problems in life are solved. How can there be a problem? A problem can't exist.

This is always because a problem is really just the lack of a viable plan. As long as we have a viable plan, there can be no problem. We know what we are going to do to tackle the problem. There is an obstruction in life, no problem. We have a viable plan to overcome it. So where's the problem. As long as there is a viable plan, how can there be a problem.

Once we become Karma-Yogies, we always have a viable plan. That is, we do our duty. How can we ever have a problem?

There are two really good books titled, Karma Yoga. One is by a Swami Shivananda and the other is by swami Vivekananda. Both are available for FREE on the the internet as a pdf download.

I read and reread Swami Vivekananda's, Karma Yoga, over and over about 50 times. I recommend it to anyone with problems as a way of staying detached – getting rid of all problems for good. For the past almost 50 years, since I first started practicing Karma Yoga, I have had no problems. My friends all get angry with me when I say this. But again, they don't practice Karma Yoga and don't know this is possible, I forgive them.

Detachment (Scientifically letting go) is the answer to problems when life goes wrong! By analyzing, we find doing our duty in life is always a viable plan, because after we've done everything to bring good results. There's simply nothing more to be done. We've done our duty and dedicated the results to God? We can be 100% successful at doing this.

Because our selfishness and self-centeredness never really disappears until enlightenment, problems do arise frequently. The solution is always the same: Karma Yoga – 1, Take refuge in Deity of choice. 2, go to work for Deity, praying only for the knowledge of their will for us and the power to carry that out. And 3, dedicate the fruits of actions – never taking personal credit or blame for the success or failure. Then where's the problem?

We do our duty which is to please God and those around us. As such, the problem dissolves into a space-like vacuity and is gone. The problem is replaced with the viable play: that is, we do our duty in life. Whatever the future holds: that is, success or failure, we maintain our state of mind with dignity, honor and peace of mind. So where is the problem? When this happens, it's

LOGICALLY impossible for a problem to exist.

Quote from the book, Karma Yoga by Swami Vivekananda: "Buddha said, 'I do not care to know your various theories about God. What is the use of discussing all the subtle doctrines about the soul? Do good and be good. And this will take you to freedom and to whatever TRUTH there is. .... 'He (the Buddha) is the ideal Karma Yogi, acting entirely without (personal) motive (detached), and the history of humanity shows him to have been the greatest man ever born; beyond compare the greatest combination of heart and brain that ever existed, the greatest soul-power that has ever been manifested. He is the first great reformer the world has seen. 'He was the first who dared to say, "Believe not because some old manuscripts are produced, believe not because it is your national belief, because you have been made to believe it from your childhood; but reason it all out, and after you have analyzed it, then, if you find that it will do good to one and all, believe it, live up to it, and help others to live up to it. 'He works best who works without any (personal) motive (detached), neither for money, nor for fame, nor for anything else; and when a man can do that, he will be a Buddha, and out of him will come the power to work in such a manner as will transform the world. This man represents the very highest ideal of Karma-Yoga.'"

God speaks to us many ways. It may be through scripture, a preacher or even a friend with an encouraging word or two. But mostly I believe God speaks to us in terms of common sense and reason. And that is certainly true of Karma Yoga. Praying only for the knowledge of God's will for me and the power to carry that out, I believe my prayers are answered.

Based on common sense and reason, I believe God tells us personally exactly what to do. Once the problem is analyzed, a viable common sense plan usually always arises. And when this doesn't happen, based on logic and reason, doing our duty is the only thing left to do logically that makes any sense.

Consequently Karma Yoga always provides a common sense viable plan. So then where's the problem? Thus I have been able to avoid all problems for the past almost 50 years.

The psychiatrist, Dr. Karl Jung writes: "Talk as much as you want, isolate yourself continuously, still this 'I' (the ego – the cause of all mental pain and suffering) will always return to you. Cut down the poplar tree today and you will find tomorrow it forms new shoots. When you find that this 'I' (the ego or selfishness and self-centeredness) cannot be destroyed, let it remain as 'I,' the servant (of God or Ultimate Reality)." (From Volume 11 of Jung's Collected Works, published by Princeton University Press, in the foreword to Der Weg Zum Selbest.)

Karma Yoga
Most Important Of All Virtues

Dedicating the Fruits (results of actions – good or bad) to our highest ideal or God can lead directly to enlightenment. Whereas all the other virtues lead only to the middle path of dignity, honor and peace of mind. Other virtues also provide good karma. But dedicating the Fruits of actions to the Lord, or other, is beyond all karma. It's a way of renouncing the conceptual dualities of life. Enlightenment or realizing Emptiness, Brahman, Divine Mind, etc. involves going beyond all concepts, especially the concepts of good and bad. Therefore, Karma Yoga leads directly to enlightenment. So when the mind goes into a space like vacuity as explained in following chapters from practicing Karma Yoga, it's actually a realization of Emptiness or Brahman, etc. And since this doesn't happen with any of the other virtues based on the author's personal experience and opinion, this makes Karma Yoga the most important virtue of them all.

Nagarjuna writes in the 25th Chapter of Fundamental Principles, "As for those still trapped in the concepts of good and bad, I pity the fools."

One (1) Negative to Karma Yoga

There is only one negative to Karma Yoga. It puts our minds into the state of Rajas. Oddly enough, once we began practicing Karma Yoga, we achieve greater success in everything. Consequently it's hard not to take personal credit for this. As a result, our egos get way out of hand. Karma Yoga makes a person that successful, it's practically impossible to be humble.

Unfortunately this puts the mind in Rajas. As such, we have an abundance of physical and mental energy to accomplish outstanding works. Because we are now in the mind set of *Rajas,* fear and depression do not arise. That's good! But the bad part of *Rajas* is anger. This makes it also necessary to practice Meeta (antidote for Anger) in order to roll the mind back into the middle path of Sattva where spiritual growth takes place and authentic worldly happiness abides. See Sublimation, Part Two (2) for instructions for practicing Meeta, the easy way to end anger.

Understanding Ontology

Part 1

This section is totally necessary!
Do not move on until you
understand it perfectly!

The book, Fundamental Principles Of The Middle way, points to one fact and one fact only. The evolution of the world, as we know it, could not have taken place through cause and affect. Yes, the testimony of our senses tells us that cause and affect is very real, and anyone who might doubt it, has been sadly misinformed. We are even taught in school that every legitimate cause leads to it's scientific effect – or so it appears! All of the sciences like math, biology, physics, chemistry, etc are based upon cause and effect. No change takes place without a cause which evolves to an effect – or so it seems.

In rebuttal the ontologist might ask, "Which came first the chicken or the egg?"

Tracing it back, we get an infinite regression. That is, we can not come up with a scientifically sound answer to which came first. It takes and egg to get a chicken but it also takes a chicken to get an egg. Therefore, it's impossible to find an original cause.

The religionists claim, "God was the original cause of the chicken or chickens that began laying eggs.

But this answer is not satisfying to the scientist, who then asks, "Who made God?" And since there is not an original cause to have produced God, the ontologist says, "Even God did not evolve through cause and effect.

And besides, if God did make everything, it still can't work based on cause and affect. And so the ontologist asks, in the 21st

Century – now that God made everything – which comes first, the father or the child? Everyone says, "The father comes first."

But this can't be! "A father can't be a father until first there is a child." Therefore, the father can't come first!

Which comes first, the spark or the explosion? "We all say the spark!" But the correct answer is, the spark can't be the spark that actually caused the explosion until first there is an explosion. Therefore, the ontologist says, cause and affect is an illusion. In both of the above examples, the effect: that is, the child and the explosion precede their cause. Both defy logic and reason. Therefore, cause and affect as well as everything it produces is an illusion, unreal, like something that happens in dreams.

Greek, Buddhist, and Hindu Ontology provides a much better theory about how the universe began. It does not take sides. This theory is a middle path between cause and effect on one side, and God on the other. This is because it provides not only a logical scientific theory for those who believe in God. It also offers a logical scientific theory for those who do not believe in God.

How the world began seems like idle information developed by an idle curiosity. And as far as the information being of any real use for the average person, seem totally unlikely. Instead this information is intensely useful. It is the most practical information in the universe. This is because once it's realized, it's NOT possible to experience any suffering.

This ontological theory is, the world is an illusion. It's not real! Nobody made it. And cause and effect can't take place. Logically neither God, nor man, nor magicians – not anybody can make something from nothing. Theoretically and originally our entire cosmos was a void. Nothing existed! Yes, there is the big bang theory of the scientists.

Before that there was no time, no space, no causation and no atoms. The ontologist says, this is still true. This argument doesn't deny the existence of God – only that creation doesn't continue by means of cause and affect. And at the same time, it doesn't require a god for it's existence. If you believe in God, that's fine. And if you don't believe in God, that's fine too.

The scientific theory of creation is what causes suffering. The scientists claim the world is real. The ontologist claims it isn't. For them how it all began is not necessary. Only that cause and affect, as we know it, can not take place, never took place and will never take place. This supposedly real existence of our normal waking state of consciousness is not real. It's like an illusion – like our experience in dreams. The illusion is, everything exists outside our mind in a real world. Instead it all happens inside our minds, like dreams.

When we are dreaming and have a nightmare, we are very upset – emotionally distraught! We might be angry, fearful, greedy, depressed or guilty. Why? Because we think our dream is real. While we are dreaming we don't know the dream is unreal. We believe it's actually happening. But as soon as we wake up, all emotional pain ends with the realization, it's only a dream.

The reason this information is intensely practical is because it offers a way to end all suffering. And if our ontological realization progresses beyond the information in this book, that only deals with emotional pain, we can end all suffering – not just our emotional pain.

PrajanaParamita
Scriptures

Nagarjuna got most of his inspiration for Fundamental Principals in the First Century from what are called the *PrajanaParamita* (Sanskrit) Scriptures which had been lost for about 500 years since the time of Buddha, when Nagarjuna, himself, re-discovered them.

Prajana means highest wisdom which is ecstatic bliss. We can partially find this *prajana* many mornings when we wake up. It is the bliss of sleep which is a formless realm. During sleep we have no perception of forms. Dreaming sleep is of course a form realm wherein we see many dream forms. But dreamless sleep is a blissful formless realm. Dreamless sleep is a pain free realm. We can go to sleep with both physical and emotional pain. When we wake up, we realize that while we were sleeping (dreamless), we did not experience any physical or emotional pain. Most of us have already recognized this fact from our own experience.

It's because of this *prajana* bliss that we are reluctant to get up some mornings. Rather than face the cruel world, we cling to the bliss and will not let go. In fact it hurts to leave this formless realm and venture up into the form filled world of seemingly cause and affect. We always know how we've slept. Upon awakening we can follow our consciousness back, eventually into the bliss of dreamless sleep. Only sometimes it's a disturbed state because of restless dreams which we mostly don't remember.

It is this *prajana* or highest bliss that most Eastern type of meditation wish to experience. It involves stilling the breath which in turn stills the mind. One way to do this is to simply watch the breath and it will slow down as we relax into *prajana* bliss. Once the mind slows, as we near the formless state, all emotional pain gradually ceases.

Dreamless sleep is also a healing state and so is meditation when the breath is calmed. Once we are adept in a few weeks or months, we will be able to purge a cold or a simple headache simply by meditating – simply by calming the mind: that is, by calming the breath.

Paramita means the practice of certain virtues. Please note that the virtues presented in Sublimation 1, 2, 3 & 4 are sufficient for Killing all emotional pain immediately. But other virtues – not given in this text are said to be necessary to gain full enlightenment.

Enlightenment which is the end of all suffering, requires a thing called *bodhichitta* in Sanskrit which means, "The intellectual mind stuff that causes enlightenment." *Bodhichitta* is of two kinds, conventional and ultimate. Both *bodhichittas* are required. In the same way both wings of a bird are necessary in order to fly. One wing alone is not enough. One kind of *bodhichitta* is not enough.

Conventional *bodhichitta* are the *paramitas* or virtues that sublimate all emotional pain immediately. And ultimate bodhichittas is the ontological arguments which causes the mind to reveal the non-affirming negative called Emptiness, Brahman, Divine Mind, etc. – the true nature of reality.

Although this book is not about religion and deals mainly with killing all emotional pain immediately. The process of ontological physical healing is the same. Christian Science uses Bible passages to convince the mind: that is, all sickness and discord are NOT real. Nagarjuna's Fundamental Principles of the Middle Way uses logic and reason to prove the exact same thing. That is, all sickness and discord are NOT real. Once the mind is convinced that all suffering is not real, the suffering vanishes immediately. This is true of emotional suffering and it's also true of physical suffering. In the same way, we end all suffering caused by a nightmare when we realize the nightmare isn't real.

Healing all emotional pain immediately is easier, but the

same ontological arguments can be used to prove that physical illness isn't real also. However, physical healing takes greater effort and longer periods of time. Therefore, physical healing will also be discussed.

Understanding Ultimate Reality!

Hindu Advaita Vedanta and Mahayana Buddhism are quite similar in their description of Ultimate Reality. This is understood by examining two (2) metaphysical Sanskrit terms that are common to both religions. N*am* means, "Name," and *rupa* means, "Form, but it is written N*amarupa.* It's the 4th link in the Buddhist system of Dependent Arising. All 12 links crumble into emptiness or Brahman (Ultimate Reality) especially by understanding this 4th link, *namarupa.*)

The scientific philosophy of *namarupa* is that the physical world, as we know it, is not substantial or physical. Instead it's only name and form (*namarupa*). Although it appears inherently real, it is not. Another term is also helpful. It's the English word, "Metaphysical," which means: anything that is NOT physical.

Conventionally, everything that exists in the universe is either physical or metaphysical. There is no third choice. Yes the universe exists but is it physical or metaphysical? Everyone answers, "Physical!" That's only until it's examined scientifically. As the universe appears to our senses, it's physical. But ontologists tell us differently. Yes it all exists, but based on the intelligence of our mind, it doesn't exist as it appears.

In our normal waking state of consciousness we are mistaken. The analogy is seeing a piece of rope on our path but mistaking it for a snake. In this case the rope that is mistaken for a snake would be *namarupa*: that is, only name and form. The rope snake is totally unreal. What we think is a real snake when examined closely is realized to be unreal: that is, only like a piece of rope.

Let's examine a forest. Yes, the forest exists but how does it exist? Is it physical or metaphysical? We naturally say the forest is physical. In order for a forest to be real and not just a name, it would have to be the same as the clump of threes. In that case the forest and the trees would exist from their own side somewhere outside of our own mind. (Please note: a name can only exist inside our mind)

If the forest and trees did exist outside our mind, then we could easily find them where they're supposed to be, and we could agree the forest is real. But we shall show it's not possible to find either the forest or the trees as something other than names and forms (*namarupa*) which exists solely inside our own mind.

We mistakenly think that the forest is the same as the clump of trees. But the word, forest, is not the same as the clump of trees. Grammatically the forest possesses the trees. We write this, "The forest's trees."

The apostrophe "s," in forest's shows that the forest possesses the trees. There must be two aspects with every possessor. Firstly there is the possessor and secondly there is the possesse. And each must be different. Clearly the possessor must be different from the possesse. The possessor is an owner. Owner involves two aspects: that is, the owner (forest) and the owned (trees). So clearly the forest is not the same as the trees which it possesses or owns.

So where does the forest exist? Logically and clearly there is only one place for it to exist: that is, a name inside our own mind. And since it's different from the trees it possesses or owns, we logically and clearly can NOT find any forest from the side of the trees – where the forest is supposed to be. This proves it's only *namarupa*!

But we can reach out with our hand and actually touch the trees. But how can we touch a forest which doesn't really exist, it's only a word – a name. How can we touch a name inside our own mind?

But how about the trees themselves? Can we reach out and touch them! They seem like something physical but are they? We find that a single tree is exactly like the forest. It's only a name for certain parts that go to make up what is commonly known as a tree. Can we reach out and touch the tree? NO! What we think we are touching is only the parts of a tree. And like the forest, the tree is only a name – different from it's parts because it possess or owns them. Therefore, the tree, itself, is only a name inside our mind. It does not actually exist where it's supposed to be. The tree also can not be found in the outside world. We never find the possessor of the parts. We only find and touch the parts.

How about the parts of the tree which also possess or own it's parts. A leaf for example is only a name for the cellulose and minerals that go to make up what is called a leaf. A leaf possesses or owns it's parts, so it too exists only as a name inside our own

mind. That is, we can 't reach out and touch the leaf itself – only
the parts. And the same is true for all the parts of the parts of
everything in the universe. Nothing can be found anywhere from
it's own side, it's all a conceptual fabrication of our own mind –
namarupa!

Meditation on *Namamupa*
Name and Form!

For this meditation we concentrate on our own body. Is our
own body inherently real. Can we find this body where we expect
to find it: that is, where it's supposed to be, outside of our own
mind? Or is it also only name and form: that is, a conceptual
fabrication of our own mind?

If our body was the same as it's parts, we could find it
where it's supposed to be. And we could all agree it's something
real. But if it's not the same as it's parts, that's not going to happen.
Grammatically we write it, "The Body's parts." The apostrophe
"s," signifies the Body's ownership of it's parts. Consequently,
logically and clearly the body must be different from it's parts. The
possessor must be different from the possesses. In the same way
the owner must be different from the owned. So since the body
owns or possesses it's parts, it must be different. And we are not
able to find it from the side where the body is supposed to be.

That's because the body, too, is a conceptual fabrication of
our own mind – based upon the body's parts – NOT inherently real
– something metaphysical – only *namarupa*! It exists only in our
mind – something like a dream tree.

When we look for our hand, we find the same thing. The
hand is only a name for a clump of parts including the fingers,
knuckles, nails etc. And since it's different from it's parts, we will
not be able to find our hand where it's supposed to be. It, too, exists
as a name and form – conceptually fabricated – based on it's parts
– in our own mind.

And when we check all the parts of our body, we find there
is nothing to be found from its' own side. It's all name and form,
conceptually fabricated in our own mind. Nothing about our body
is inherently real.

Stephen Hawking who once had the same job as Sir Issac
Newton at Cambridge University, said that once matter can be
fully examined beyond, atoms, electrons, etc, the tiniest of

unnamed divisions can be perceived. According to him, it's something resembling thought.

Yes, our body exists, but it's NOT inherently real. A dream exists but it, too, is NOT inherently real. A dream only exists as something conceptually fabricated in our own mind. Logically we prove the body does exist. How can our body not exist? We see it touch it, etc. What are we proving? That, our body is NOT inherently real.

In this meditation it's possible to negate the wrong thing. That is, we might negate the existence of the body itself. If we did, this realization would be called Nihilism: that is, that nothing exists in the universe.

This is a wrong view but it happens routinely on this path. In this case, the meditator's body as well as the universe and everything in it mistakenly dissolves into nothingness (this according to Jefferey Hopkins, Emptiness Yoga 1987). Because of this fact, the philosophy of Nihilism (belief that nothing exists ultimately) emerges.

Negating inherent reality, a non-affirming negative emerges which is called Emptiness, Brahman, Divine Mind, Ultimate Reality, etc. It can NOT be expressed verbally because there are no words in any language to describe it. However, it can be realized inferentially using the above logic. The highest realization is a direct realization.

For example, when we see smoke coming from a chimney, we inferentially realize there must be a fire in the fireplace, furnace, etc. But when we go inside and actually see the fire, this is a direct experience. So a direct experience of an Ontological Truth is what we are after, but this takes a very long time. In the meantime a simple inferential realization will kill all emotional pain immediately. And it will kill physical suffering too.

Both Mahayana Buddhists and Advaita Vedantists are Monists. In this case Ultimate Reality happens when the observer and the knowledge of the observation are realized to be the same: that is, everything becomes one. Otherwise Monism – by definition – can't happen. Therefore, Mahayana Buddhists and Advaita Vedantists share the same Ultimate Direct Realization of Reality: that is, Monism. They differ only so far as the description of the experience is concerned.

Mahayana Buddhists say, the universe exists only

conventionally, but ultimately it neither exists nor does it not exist (a middle path: that is, something between realism and nihilism). From this same realization of Monism, the Hindu Advaita Vedantists say, Ultimate Reality is Sat-Chit-Ananda: that is, Pure Existence, Pure Consciousness, and Pure Bliss. But are these two definitions really different? If both are Monists, how can they be different? Explaining ultimate reality fully gets very complicated, so it will not be explained further until Chapter 25.

All that's really required to end all emotional pain immediately is sublimation and or an inferential ontological realization of ultimate reality. All is based on logic and reason – not on religious superstition or anything else.

Antidote For Catastrophic Illness

In 2007 I was in China with the Swine flu. I was so sick, I thought I would die. I could not even get out of bed to visit the toilet. I used the *namarupa* meditation in order to get relief. Believing my body was nothing more than name and form, I let go totally and was blessed with a Samadhi experience. Everything dissolved into oneness: that is, me, the meditation, and everything in the universe all became one. And all was colored with a taste of the BodhiSattva Tsongkhapa.

It was a Direct experience of Emptiness on Third (3rd) Path. But at the same time, since the universe disappeared, it was a wrong view. This means the realization on the Third (3rd) Path is different from the final and correct view of Emptiness on the Fifth (5th) Path Of No More Learning. But it had one tremendous advantage.

I was able to dissolved the Swine flu into nothingness. It was impossible to believe I was either sick or that my body actually existed. In fact, nothing in the universe existed. I completely lost consciousness of the universe and everything around me in total Nihilism. Only my experience of oneness was there.

But my mind was wide awake in a formless realm of Supreme Prajana Bliss. Instead of being a direct view of Emptiness, I believe it was a Direct realization of the formless sleep realm only. The experience lasted for about 20 minutes. I would love to get this experience anytime I wanted but no. It has only been granted several dozen times. The real fun of this experience was that we stop breathing altogether in Super-Consciousness or Samadhi. After about 20 minutes of not breathing, I was NOT even slightly grasping for air. There was pure and total infallible peace. This was the greatest experience of well-being ever.

When the mind goes into Samadhi (Divine consciousness), all breathing stops totally. I consider this normal. This has happened dozens of times before. But this was the only time it happened when I was really sick. The other fun part of this experience was that I was immediately and completely cured of my Swine Flu. I was suddenly instantly well.

What I think cured me was the thought that neither my body nor the swine flu existed. Either that or it was the the Prajana Bliss which engulfed me like a Divine Mother with supernatural love and healing.

I had places to go that afternoon which required my walking about five (5) miles. I do not mean that I felt better or that my illness had greatly improved. I mean my Swine flu was completely gone! The Swine Flu did not come back the following morning. It did not come back ever.

Even though the *namarupa* realization of emptiness is not a final and highest view, it has three (3) main advantages. First it will kill all emotional pain immediately. Second, it will convince us that the universe and everything in it is only name and form: that is, nothing really exists inherently. And third (3), since physical illness is nothing more than name and form, it also does not really exist. And when this happens, physical healing will actually take place.

But we don't need a Samadhi experience of *namarupa* in order for healing to take place. Unless we go into Samadhi, the physical healing may not be instantaneous. However, a *namarupa* inferential realization will always help us feel better, and then ultimately healing will take place more rapidly.

Namarupa meditation answers the question, what is sickness? Does it exist physically? Or does it exist metaphysically? All sickness possesses or owns it's symptoms. That means that the sickness itself is not the same as it's symptoms. If the symptoms were the same as the sickness, we could find the sickness in our body. Yes we do find the sickness, but it's in our mind and not where it's supposed to be: that is, inside our body. All sickness is, therefore, an illusion, like the body, like the trees, like the forest, like everything.

The logical question during the meditation is, if the sickness only exists as a conceptual fabrication of our own minds (*namarupa* – name and form), how can we really be sick?

Our thoughts convincing us that our sickness isn't real is the cure. And besides, if the body doesn't really exist, how can I really be sick anyway? This logic, too, is the cure.

However, using this same meditation for emotional pain is far easier and quicker. All emotional pain ends once the bliss of *prajana* arises. This happens in meditation when the non-affirming negative arises: that is, we actually understand the body isn't inherently real. Once the emotional pain disappears into the space like vacuity, and the bliss of *prajana* takes over, all emotional pain is gone. Additionally we feel better, and best of all, actual healing takes place more quickly. What might have taken weeks to heal, may take only a few days because of the inferential realization. A common cold that takes seven days to recover from, can be gone in a single day.

The Hindu Mandukya Upanishad mentions three states of consciousness that everyone knows about: that is, normal waking state, dreamless sleep and dreaming sleep. Beyond that, there is *Turiya* (Sanskrit) the fourth state wherein Ultimate Reality or realization of Brahman happens. *Prajana* is used to define the sleep state in the Mandukya Upanishad. That is, the highest wisdom is to be found in the bliss of dreamless sleep.

It is the writer's personal experience that this highest *prajana* bliss can be realized without losing consciousness during dreamless sleep. The meditation to accomplish this is *namarupa*. All that's necessary is to dissolve the body into a space like vacuity and hold it into sleep. All awareness of body consciousness is lost – just like normal sleep – but the mind is super awake in *prajana*. A thousand bottles of whiskey can't compare to the intoxication which is pure pleasure.

Ontology Must Be Realized!

It does no good at all to just memorize the ontological arguments, like any scientist learning formulas in a secular university. Just memorizing the arguments will not kill any emotional pain. That's because ontology must be realized in order to scientifically let go of our emotional pain: that is, to scientifically kill the suffering. The ontological arguments have to be realized, visualized, and understood at a deep level, etc.

There is a true and terrible story about Galileo who wrote a book about 500 years ago. This story describes how realization is not only important for ontology but also it can be important for the physical sciences as well. Galileo's book said, the sun revolves around the earth. This contradicts the testimony or our senses. We do actually see the sun rising in the east and setting in the west.

Galileo was not the first person to present this science. There was an ancient Greek who also said the same thing. But 500 years ago was during the time of the Spanish Inquisition. The bible says in Ecclesiastes 1:5, "The sun rises and the sun goes down, and hastens to the place where it rises."

Thus Galileo was condemned by the Inquisition to life imprisonment for writing something that disagreed with the Bible. His sentence was partially commuted a year later. Instead he was actually forced to spend the remaining 12 years of life under house arrest in his home.

Even more amazingly is the fact that 25% of the people in USA today get it wrong. One in four still believes erroneously that the sun revolves around earth. The reason for this is obvious. He or she must have learned the facts in school but never took the time to actually visualize, realize or actually understand this science.

They probably did not sit down and visualized the earth in it's orbit: that is, the sun standing relatively still in our solar system, and the earth spinning on it's axis around the sun at about a thousand mile per hour. If they had done this, they would have gotten it right thereafter.

In the writer's own experience, I never believed this as a kid. I thought they were trying to play a joke on me, like Santa Clause who went around to all the good children with presents in a single night, Christmas eve. I knew this couldn't happen since there are way too many children for one (1) Santa to visit in a single night.

First off, I couldn't imagine the world as round or oval shaped. I saw it as flat. And I saw the earth standing still with the sun moving across the sky in a single day. Later in high school during eighth (8th) grade science class, I came to understand the earth did actually revolved around the sun – not the other way around. It was no joke. The sun and earth did actually behave that way.

But I could not do this without first setting it up in my own mind inferentially. Then I actually realized it. I visualized the earth as round and that the earth did revolve around the sun. Still the testimony of my senses gave me the false information that the earth was flat – not round. But instead of accepting the false information from the testimony of my senses, I reaffirmed the scientific concept again and again.

Killing all emotional pain immediately is exactly like this. The ontological arguments have to be reaffirmed again and again. The knowledge of he testimony of our senses has to be proven false time and time again. And when this happens again and again, the mind finally gets convinced again and goes into a space like vacuity, killing all emotional pain immediately – convincing us the universe and everything is an illusion, like a dream, unreal, etc.

Hong Sau Method of Meditation

The Bhagavad Gita, verse 4: 29 says, the breath can be stopped totally. But this doesn't happen with will power. This technique is taught fully in Raja Yoga (Royal Yoga) lessons taught through the mail by Self Realization Fellowship (SRF). I studied these lessons in about 1970 for a few years. Before taking these lessons, it's necessary to sign a pledge not to disclose any information in the lessons.

I will, however, partially describe one of the techniques for meditation, because it's also used by others, and it's good to learn. Hopefully, SRF will not be too angry with me.

Sit in a chair with legs straight, bent at the knees, and feet flat on the floor. Head, neck, and back in a straight line making a, "h," with the floor.

This position was too hard on my back. After about ten (10) minutes, my back hurt so badly I could not continue.

I solved this problem entirely by leaning forward slightly. This combined with other SRF instructions, "Hands should be resting on knees with palms of hands turned upwards," made a firm support for my back. By leaning forward slightly against my hands on the knees and palms turned upward, it created a firm support for the body. In this position, the body did not fall over – even when I fell asleep very occasionally with long 5 hour meditations. My head slumped forward, but the body, itself, did not fall over.

Then finally I wondered if I died in this position, my head might slump forward, but would my body ever fall over? Probably never, I thought, until it decomposed and turned to dust.

I sat in a chair but I crossed my lower legs, like one might sit in a cross legged (lotus position or American Indian position if I were sitting on the floor.) Since I was sitting on a chair, my lower legs were crossed so my feet were turned to the sides – not flat on the floor according to SRF instructions. This, too, was to strengthened my meditation position so I could not fall over.

I was asked why I just didn't sit in a lotus position. Because I couldn't – too hard on my knees.

It took about 1 year to actually get comfortable with this position. When the position got too unbearable, I retreated to a comfortably cushioned chair. I made the effort for only 15 minutes a day. Today, I can sit this way for hours – but only by leaning forward on my hands and my feet folded under me – not as originally taught by SRF.

Repeat the Sanskrit mantra, *"Hong – Sau." Hong* is pronounced as it's written. *Sau* is pronounced like the English word, "Sow," which means a female mother pig. But it rhymes with cow.

With mouth closed, as the breath comes in normally through the nostrils, chant, "Hong," and as the breath flows out normally through the nostrils, chant, "Sau." Do not try to stop the breath in any way. At the same time, keep the attention at a single point slightly above and between the eyebrows called the spiritual eye.

Calm the mind: that is, suppress all thoughts by not paying attention to them. Think of your thoughts as rising like waves in the sea and receding as they disappear in the ocean and then new waves (thoughts) arise. At the same time refrain from adding any additional thoughts, but always keep watching the breath. Watching the breath and repeating the mantra is what calms the mind and so the breath will become slower and slower.

Pranayama
(Sanskrit)

The main aspect of relaxation is not only breath control but also to make sure both nostrils are taking in air at the same rate. The technique for doing this is:

1, Close mouth. Close right nostril with a finger and gently and slowly inhale air deeply through the left nostril until full. Then close the left nostril and gently and slowly completely exhale breath thoroughly through right nostril.

2, Still covering left nostril, gently and slowly inhale deeply through the right nostril. Then cover the right nostril with finger, and gently and slowly exhale through left nostril until all air is expended.

1, and 2, combined equal one repetition. Do five (5) repetition. If air is not going through each nostrils equally, do more than five (5) repetitions but not more than twenty (20). From this we learn that we rarely breathe evenly through each nostril until after we do this meditation.

At the end of our meditation, the best check to see if we relaxed into the meditation is to do one complete round of *pranayama.* Does the air enter each nostril equally and flow evenly? Or is one nostril still taking in more air? If both nostrils are taking in air evenly and equally, the meditation was successful.

At the time of my Samadhi experiences where the breath stopped totally for long periods of time, I was practicing *Hong / Sau* meditation 5 hours a day.

SRF teaches that one (1) hour of this meditation is the same as doing 24 hours or longer of any other kind of mediation. Therefore, I thoroughly encourage everyone to do this meditation at least 30 minutes every morning and 30 minutes every night. Once the breath slows way down, and both nostrils are taking in and exhaling air equally, we reach a point called, "Calm Abiding." Here subtler minds which are more intelligent take over and the discursive reasoning for the ontological meditations will not disturb the depth of our meditation.

This is the first advantage of slowing the breath with this meditation. The second advantage is *prajana,* the partially pure pleasure of a supernatural peace and bliss which pervades our being, is the second advantage.

The mantra, *Hong / Sau* means many things in Sanskrit: that is, "I am He," "I am That," "I am God," "I am Emptiness," "I am Brahman," etc. The meanings, however, are not so important. This is because the Sanskrit words themselves have been selected to calm the mind. Just repeating these words will have a special calming affect upon the mind – no matter how they're interpreted. It doesn't matter what they mean.

If the above mantra words of *Hong Sau* is objectionable, use any one of the following:

The Buddha's mantra: *Om Muni Muni Maha Muni ye Soha*
Manjurshi's mantra: *Om, A, Ra, Pa, Sta Na, Dhi*
Heart Sutra mantra: *Tayatha Om Gaté Gaté Paragaté*
Parasamgaté Bodhi Svaha!

The Heart Sutra mantra has a purely secular meaning "Gone, gone, gone to the other shore beyond." Again the meaning is not so important. The main advantage is the Sanskrit words that calm the mind. Any and all of these mantras will have a calming affect on the mind.

Or use any mantra. Giving the mind something to do is a way of partially discouraging thought from arising.

An Old Wives Tale

Tradition has it, once a person has a direct experience of n*amarupa*, this ultimately breaks the chain of Buddha's 12 links of Dependent Arising. And although a person is not totally enlightened by it, he or she will have broken this cycle of birth and death. Consequently they will not be reborn in *samskara* ever again. Thus he or she will have the privilege to work on enlightenment in a Pure Land on higher planes of existence. Or there is a choice to reincarnate into the earth plane again as a Bodhisattva.

Alternative Meditation

There are times when the above meditation of concentrating at the spiritual eye – slightly above the eyebrows, gets strained. Many times a pain arises there and to continue in this mediation means enduring actual physical pain. When this pain can't be turned into infallible peace with one of the ontological meditations, there's a different approach.

Concentration at the point between the eyebrows is only one of the *chakaras* (Sanskrit). There are several: that is, at the top of the head, the spiritual eye, the throat *chakara*, the heart *chakara* (center of the chest between the nipples), navel *chakara, etc.*

If the spiritual eye becomes too painful, it's best to use another *chakara.* The Heart *chakara* is another good place.

There is also a mystical central channel in Buddhism that is about the size of the middle finger and runs mostly in a straight line from the top of the head (crown *chakara*) to the tip of the sex organ. The inside of this channel is a gorgeous and soothing oily red color inside and pale blue outside. Inside it's this beautiful oily red somewhat like blood. It's very clear and transparent. And it's very soft and flexible like a lotus petal.

It runs through the center of the body but sightly to the back and stands directly in front of another mystical channel called the life channel or *sushumna* (Sanskrit) used by the Raja Yogies, which is behind and near the spinal column.

Should the spiritual eye get too painful, use the following alternative meditation. Use the heart *chakara*. From there go up and down the central channel visualizing the color and texture. Moving from the crown *chakara* to the heart chakara and then to the tip of the sex organ – up and down until the prajana bliss is restored.

Or concentrate only on the heart *chakara* repeating one of the mantras. The central channel has been for me a very safe and pleasurable experience. Moving inside the *sushumna* was not really a great experience without a Raga Yogi Guru.

Disclaimer

The meditations on *namarupa* clearly explains conventional reality: that is, what's at the core of self-grasping ignorance (the cause of all suffering) It's an involuntary kind of grasping, possession, or ownership. *Namarupa* is one of the best ways to scientifically let go.

Chapter 10 of Fundamental Principals, however, teaches that it is impossible for anything to possess or own it's parts. It also teaches that the self is the same as the aggregates and at the same time different from them. Nothing real can exist this way. Therefore, it proves that everything is just appearance – appearance emptiness.

But does Chapter 10 actually contradict the *namarupa* meditation describing possession? The answer is no. This is true because they both teach emptiness form different perspectives.

Chapter 10 teaches *samskara* is unreal because, nothing can be the same and different at the same time. The *namarupa* meditation teaches that the actual existence of everything is inside our mind and not outside where it seemingly appears.

The *namarupa* meditation is actually taught in Chapter 20, An Examination of Collections. If Nagarjuna believed they were a contradiction, he would not have included Chapter 20. Therefore, Chapter 10 and Chapter 20 do not contradict each other.

Understanding Ontology

Part 2

This section is totally necessary!
Do not move on until you
understand it perfectly!

The Emptiness of Time
Time, Like Everything Else, it's An Illusion!
Realizing This Will Kill All Emotionally Immediately!

There is a conventional way and ontological way of viewing time that will kill all emotional pain immediately. Both methods compliment each other. Using the conventional method first, we discover most emotional pain happens because we are either thinking about the past or the future.

Seven (7) Truth Aphorisms
Concerning Conventional Time
And Emotional Pain
Easily Proven in the Laboratory of Our Lives

1, Emotional pain arises in the so-called present because of something that happens conventionally now.
2, Otherwise, emotional pain arises in the so called present by thinking of the past. We are never in the past, it doesn't exist as a place in time for us. The past only exists in the so-called present while we are thinking about the past.
3, Or otherwise, emotional pain arises in the so-called present by thinking about the future. We are never actually in the future, it doesn't exist as a place in time for us. The future also exists in the so-called present while we are thinking

about the future.

4, Conventionally there is no other way for Emotional pain to arise. All emotional pain arises in the so called present. It is always the present – never the future or the past.

5, Almost all emotional pain (99.99%) of it happens when we think about the past or the future.

6, This is because if something does happen in the so called present to cause emotional pain, a fraction of a second later it's the past. That is, we are only in the so-called present for a fraction of second until it becomes the past.

7, That means practically NO emotional pain is possible when we control our mind by concentrating only on the conventional here and now: that is, the so-called present – neither thinking about the past or the future – not even very slightly!

First meditation:
Examining The Above Facts
Until Logically
They Make Sense To Us

It does no good to just memorize the above aphorisms. They must be analyzed and understood by personal experience. There was a Best Seller, The Power of Now by Eckart Tolle 1997. By inquiry, or *vichara* (Sanskrit), we must determine these facts to be true for ourselves.

We must analyze time in the laboratory of our own life. By doing this, we can understand by personal observation that all seven (7) of the above aphorisms are True. We must be able to thoroughly understand how it's possible for a catastrophe to occur in the so-called present, which only lasts for a fraction of a second, and how one person might suffer emotional pain for only that fraction of a second. But another person might spend the rest of his or her life suffering from that same event, in that same so-called present, which also lasted only for a fraction of a second.

The most important TRUTH is the seventh (7th) aphorism: that is, "Practically no emotional pain is possible when we control our mind by concentrating only on the conventional here and now: that is, the so-called present – neither thinking about the past or the future – not even very slightly!"

Are we angry, jealous, greedy, fearful depressed, guilty, etc?

It's a fraction of a second later and the so-called present is gone. Are we still suffering emotionally?

Then we are either thinking about the past or the future. But when we bring our minds to the here and now, the so-called present, all emotional pain is gone!

By inquiry (*vichara*) into our own mind, we can come to these same conclusions based on personal experience.

Second Meditation for Killing Emotional Pain
Ontology: Realizing Time Is An Illusion!

The so-called present does not exist inherently. One reasons is because time comes and goes. From Fundamental Principals of the Middle Way, Chapter Two (2), An Examination of Coming and Going, we find there is no place for Time to arise. When we analyze time, there is either all the time that has passed in the universe. Or there is all the time yet to pass.

Where is there a place for the so-called present to arise?

All the time that has NOT passed is of course the future, which is NOT an actual place in time for us. And all the time past is of course, the past which is also NOT a place in time for us! So we've established past and future. But where's the so-called present? Logically we find no evidence of an inherently real present anywhere – not even existing for a fraction of a second!

How can this be? All emotional pain arises in the so called present along with everything else that arises. Ontologically, however, there is no real present.

If there is no place for the so-called present to arise, then why do we see it unfold second by second. It's because it's an illusion. Yes, it exists but it's not real. According to the experts, the only place for the so-called present to arise is in our own mind – the same way a dream arises. Time doesn't exist in the outside world, it only exists as an illusion inside our own mind. Yes, we think it's real.

Despite this logic, our gross material mind has doubts. It wants to accept the testimony of our senses and reject the logic of our intellect. However, in meditation, subtler minds come into play which are more intelligent. Here there can be a deep understanding, and time is seen for what it really is – something like a dream! Deep in meditation, this logic is accepted and understood. And when this happens, the mind falls into a blissful, space-like vacuity, which is an inferential realization of Emptiness that will kill all emotional pain immediately.

If we are angry, fearful, depressed or guilty, viewing the present in meditation, we realize there is no place for it to arise. How can it arise? All time that has passed is the past. Yes, we establish a past by analysis. And we can establish a future by analysis. It's all the time that has yet to pass.

But how do we establish a present. Where do we logically find it? And when we realize this, any anger that seems to have arisen vanishes! It doesn't matter what kind of emotional pain arises. It vanishes.

If we are a compulsive over-eater and the obsession to compulsively over-eat arises, it's an illusion. By realizing there is no place for desire to arise in the present, and, therefore, the desire never really arose as something inherently real, the obsession vanishes. The only way for anything, even a blade of grass, to arise is in our own mind: that is, something like the way a dream arises.

Because there is no place for anything to arise, nothing can arise as inherently real in the outside seemingly physical world.

Third Meditation On The Emptiness of Time:

There is another reason time can't logically be real. From Fundamental Principals, Chapter 19, An Examination of Time, conventional logic tells us, the present depends on the future. And the future depends on the past and the present. But in reality, for one thing to depend on another, they must both exist at the same time. Past, present, and future do not exist at the same times, so they can't logically depend on each other. Likewise emotional pain can NOT depend on events in time that can't depend on each other. This is simple logic and reason.

It's necessary to do this meditation for days or weeks – as long as it takes, usually not more than a few hours to realize these facts deep in meditation. When we get this realization one time, it becomes easier from then forward.

Third Meditation On The Emptiness of Time

In the Sutra of the Mother, the Buddha said, "The present is imperceptible. The past is imperceptible. And the future is imperceptible. Therefore, they are equality..."

Equality or sameness in a conventional sense is dull and boring. But once this pure equality or sameness of past, present and future is realized, the mind melts into a blissful, space like vacuity which is an inferential realization of Emptiness, Ontology, or Brahman that will kill all emotional pain immediately. But until we've meditated long enough to get this experience, these facts can not be applied to our own life. Therefore an actual realization is necessary.

Ultimate Reality is Emptiness, Brahman, God, etc. which never changes. In this Ultimate Reality we never change – we can NEVER be jealous, angry, fearful, depressed, guilty, etc. It's only the false ego (or carnal mind as the Christians call it) that seemingly changes to makes us angry, sad, happy, etc. But when the mind melts into this space like vacuity, we can now understand the illusion fully. That is, it must be realized.

Those who have had even an inferential realization, tell us its a blissfully happy experience in the sameness of past, present, and future. Direct Experience of Emptiness is what we are shooting for. But an inferential realization will kill all emotional pain every time. Even better is to have a Direct Experience.

While we are dreaming, we believe the dream is real. In the same way our normal waking state is really like a dream. We think a dream is real until we wake up. A direct experience of Emptiness, Brahman, God, Divine Mind etc. occurs when we have the realization without first using the inferential logic and reason to inspire us.

Someone asked the Buddha, "Are you God?"
The Buddha said, "No!"
"Then are you a saint?"
Again the Buddha said, "No."
"Then who are you?"
"I am awake," said the Buddha.

Between 1715 and 1789 – The Age Of Enlightenment – there was an attempt by Kant and others to introduce Ontology into mainstream of French thought. This attempt basically failed. Because without meditation and actual realization, it's not easy to contradict the false testimony of our senses using the logic of our intellect.

In order for ontology to work, the logic of the mind must

rule over and suppress the testimony of our senses. This is done in exactly the same way as we force the our minds to accept the truth of science. For example, we force our mind to believe the sun is relatively stationery in our solar system – not as the testimony of our senses dictates: that is, that the sun revolves around the earth.

Ontology, Emptiness, or Brahman must be realized – either inferentially which takes only a few hours in mediation. Or it can be realized directly which takes longer – years maybe? Lifetimes maybe? Both Nagarjuna, the founder of the Mahayana Buddhist tradition, and Aristotle, the Greek Philosopher, used what is called a, "Tetra-lemma," in logic to prove the world, as we know it, is not actually real. Consequently the ontology of the Greeks and the Indian Buddhists is quite similar. The Tetra-lemma will be more fully explained in Chapter 1.

Aristotle's physics (500 BC) was based on Ontology and taught in European universities as the only physics until Sir Isaac Newton developed his twelve laws of motion about 400 years ago. Ontology is still taught in European high schools. Consequently Einstein must have been exposed to ontology early in life. He too, formulated a theory that time is an illusion which is briefly explained in the following youtube.com video:

https://www.youtube.com/watch?v=VYZQxMowBsw

The Buddhist and Hindu Yogis today prove the efficacy of Ontology by becoming Siddhas: that is, we gain the ability to preform miracles. This is a side affect. The main goal is total freedom from suffering which has been achieved since earliest times.

Even Sir Isaac Newton, who was given credit for formulating certain laws of motion which are a bedrock of modern day physics, experimented extensively in metaphysics. We know this today from his library that consisted of one third (1/3) (33.3%) of books about alchemy. Newton's notes reflected that he had even been successful at metaphysically transforming gold into lead.

Since Newton was a Puritan, it would have been immoral of him to have transmuted lead into gold, so he did it the other way around – gold into lead. Most modern biographers of Newton are amazed at this fact. This is true especially because many of the books were completely hand written by Newton, himself. He spent hour after hour laboriously transcribing alchemy chants for transforming the elements from one into another.

It's also certain that Newton would have studied Aristotle's physics, since that was all that was taught at Cambridge, where Newton graduated. Newton, himself, changed all that with his own laws of motion, but it's obvious he did not abandon ontology.

Ontological logic tells us, there are certain things necessary for the universe, as we know it, to exist. These are (1) time, (2) space, (3) cause and affect, and the (4) atoms or physical matter. This has been known ontologically for probably thousands and thousands of years.

APAROKSANUBHUTI (Self-Realization {selfless self}) a book By Shankara (Tenth Century Advaita Vedantist) points to the fact that time alone is the most important factor for real existence. Verse 111 says, "That non-dual Brahman – bliss indivisible is denoted by he word, "Time." This is because it brings into present existence – in the twinkling of an eye – all beings from God the Creator down to the lowliest amoeba."

Without time, nothing can exists inherently in the universe. This is simple logic and reason. So if it turns out that time is an illusion, everything else would – by default – be an illusion: that is, nothing inherently real could exist. In the authors opinion this makes the emptiness of time one of the most important things to realize.

Another Meditation On
Ultimate Reality

Sunyta is the Sanskrit word that the Mahayana Buddhists translate as, "Emptiness," The Therevada Buddhists translate this same word from the Pali language (an ancient dialect of Sanskrit) as, "Selflessness." Emptiness may be the best terms for ultimate reality, since there is no word in any language that will describe Emptiness or Brahman. But from the standpoint of killing all emotional pain immediately, Selflessness, is a much better place to start.

This is because Selflessness describes our personal condition in relationship to ultimate Reality. If we are asked the question, who are we? The answer is, we are selfless. But how can that be? From earliest observations we conclude, we are a self. There is an observer inside all of us. As this observer observes the outside world, we are all fooled into believing – we the observer – are separate. That is, we are a self which includes our bodies and everything else as separate.

But this is a wrong analysis. Based on logic and reason, we are not separate from everything. In fact we are everything. This is because the observer never appears without it's observation. This single fact means we are not separate from our observations. If we let go of the idea that we are separate from everything, selflessness is what we would be.

If there were no self, we could not be selfish or self-centered. There could be no self-grasping ignorance. And because self-ishness and self-centeredness are the cause of all emotional suffering, there could be no emotional suffering. In order for fire to burn anything it must be different from what it consumes. That is, fire has never been known to burn itself. In order for good or bad to cause happiness or suffering, they must be different from us.

Happiness and suffering are not real which has already been stated. They are illusions which are explained in the 27 chapters of Fundamental Principles. Consequently the trick of replacing happiness and suffering with the bliss of *prajana* is what our next meditation is all about.

Meditation
On Oneness
The Proper View

We begin first by analyzing our dreams. We ourselves are the objects of our dreams. The subjects are either happiness, sadness or indifference to the events as they happen. We are a separate self and the events happen to us. This is called duality!

Once we wake up from any dream, happiness, etc. that happened is usually forgotten and we never question the subjects and objects as being separate. That's the way everything appears in our dreams, and that's the way it supposedly happens in real life. It's been mentioned before, that the observer (ourselves) never appears separately. We are never alone. We are never without an observation. This is true in our dreams as well.

So let's examine our dreams. All of the dream pictures and ourselves are a result of our own mind. This is monism. There is no duality. It's all one source, our minds. If that's the case, then everything is us: that is, our mind – ourselves are one. We who appear in the dream are our own minds. And all the dream pictures are our mind as well. We are one with everything because it's all us.

There is only one conclusion logically. We the observer

discover the knowledge of the observation and ourselves are really the same thing. In a dream, how could we be anything else? The logic is irrefutable!

But until we realize this about the waking state, this logic will do us no good.

Just thinking this way is not enough of course. This fact must be realized.

If we dreamed we were born, grew old and were about to die, would anything have actually happened inherently. Yes, it all happened, but would it be real? And if a great fear of death arose in our dream, we would suffer terribly. Yes! But would the fear be justified? Inherently nothing really happened.

If we were never really born, and we never really grew old, how could we really ever die? So no, our fear of death in dreams is not justified.

According to those who achieved enlightenment and ended suffering in their lives permanently, they tell us our (supposed) real life is exactly the same. We have never actually been born. Referring to the supposed real world, we never really grow old, and naturally we will never really die. If we have never been born, how could we ever die?

In (supposed) real life we are never alone. Our observations are always with us. As we were able to prove with our *namarupa* meditations, everything is mind which is metaphysical. It proves the (supposed) physical world doesn't exist anywhere in the outside world. It all happens inside our mind exactly like a dream. So logically, have we ever been born or grown old? And if that's true, how cold we ever die?

This too must be realized or course. In which case it's necessary for our intellect to grasp the logic and override the testimony of our senses.

When we first examine the idea of realizing everything in the outside world is actually us, this seems ridiculous. But that's exactly how things are.

We mentioned in Ontology 1, that the *namarupa* meditation did not give us a correct view of ultimate reality. Yes, it proves that nothing is real. But it also gives us the view that nothing exists. Viewing the entire universe as ourselves: that is, not different from our observations and like a dream is a proper view.

Changing to this proper view and using the emptiness of time as a meditation, it's possible not only to experience physical healing in our body, but it's also possible to kill all emotional pain immediately.

The Mahayana Buddhists have many schools. This view is from the *Madhyamaka* (Sanskrit) Tibetan School which is considered the highest realization. This is also the view of the Fourteenth (14th) Dalai Lama and the most popular. Although it may not appear to be the same view as the above meditation on dreams, the Heart Sutra says, "Form is emptiness. emptiness is form. Form is not other than emptiness and emptiness is none other than form." The commentary is that emptiness would have to be something like a dream for the Heart Sutra description to be logical.

Form is only one (1) of the five (5) aggregates or constituents of the human time, space, causation and physical matter. In Sanskrit this is called s*amskara. Sam* means joining together and *skara* means action, cause or doing. The Heart Sutra quote mentions only, "Form," but it's true of all 5 aggregates – everything we experience in life.

Mandukya Upanishad 1-14, Gaudapada's Karika, says also that our waking state is really like a dream. But it should be noted: Ultimate Reality, Emptiness, Brahman, Divine Mind, etc. is not the same as our waking, dreamless and dream states of consciousness. In fact It's not at all like anything we've experienced or could experience in *samskara*. Those enlightened tell us, NOT what Ultimate Reality Is but what it isn't. It can only be realized through meditation, and it comes in the way of a non-affirming-negative.

When we understand this, we will always be able to retreat into meditation and see the (seemingly) real world exactly like we view our dreams: that is, as something unreal, like an illusion. When this happens, all emotional pain will be gone immediately like dream suffering disappears upon awakening and realizing it was only a dream. Ultimately we will have an inferential realization first before realizing it directly. But then we will comprehend It's exact nature and only then.

One Way to Kill Depression immediately
Doing Meditation on the Emptiness of Time

Yes, we're depressed! Why? Because our lover belittled us in front of friends. He or she made a joke, informing a few friends that we didn't know how to dress correctly. We weren't expecting this and it hurt us deeply. Or supposing we are angry. Angry or depressed, it doesn't make any difference.

Our Meditation On
The Emptiness of Time

Our meditation might first involve sublimation covered in Sublimation 1, 2, 3, and 4. If we are depressed, we come up with 5 new things for which to be grateful. If we are angry, we do Meeta. And we might even take it on blind faith that the event that caused our depression was Ultimately GOOD, etc.

Or we might go immediately to an ontological meditation on the emptiness of time which would work as follows:

1, We would begin by viewing everything as ourselves, not real, like a dream.

2, Then we begin applying other logic which is, there is no place for this depression or anything else to arise. That's because there is either all the time yet to pass or there is all of the time past. This leaves no place for the depression to arise. Instead, it's all imputed just like a dream.

3, But we're still depressed. Yes, it's logical, we were belittled in the past. And since the past depends on the present where we are now depressed, our senses remind us. But since the past and the present don't exist at the same time, how is this logical? Forcing the mind to accept the logic of our intellect – not the testimony of our senses – is what kills our depression as well as all other emotional pain immediately.

When our mind falls into this space-like vacuity and depression goes immediately, it's like being inside an impregnable fortress. Noting from the outside world can touch us. This is because we see the outside world as total illusion. How can illusion hurt us? The only way illusion can hurt us is if we believe it's inherently real. Seeing it all as unreal is our protector, our fortress, and our refuge. This is called taking refuge in the Dharma (teaching of Truth).

Healing Illness
With The Emptiness of Time

Supposing we are sick, catastrophe illness or a simple headache. It doesn't matter. Using the emptiness of time to kill our illness, we use scientific logic. We ask ourselves, how can I be sick? There is either all the time remaining in the universe. And there is all the time past. Therefore, there is no place for this illness to arise. There is also no place for health to arise – no way to get well inherently.

And since past, present and future don't exist at the same times, how can they depend on each other. Again when we allow the logic of our intellect to rule over us, we kill all emotional and physical suffering. But we think we are sick at the present time. The only time the present really exists is if we are dreaming. We have logic that tells us our dreams are just like our waking state. In order to get well, we can take refuge in the Dharma. That is, we force our minds to accept the logic of our intellect and at the same time reject the testimony of our senses. When this happens, our illness will dissolve into a space-like vacuity.

The Hindu Scripture, the Bhagavad Gita says in Verse 2: 25, "We are unbreakable, and insoluble, and can neither be burned nor dried. He or she is everlasting, present everywhere, unchangeable, immovable and eternally the same."

This is not just some scripture to have faith in. The very facts of this scripture are realizable. That is, the logic of ontology can be realized inferentially very quickly – within days, weeks or months. Yes, enlightenment is a slow process that may take many lifetimes. But why wait that long. Relief comes quickly to anyone who enters the Path and is committed to these meditations.

If we are still suffering from emotional pain after a few days, weeks, or months on the spiritual path, we are not practicing correctly. Mostly it's because we are not using this logic and reason as the subject of our meditations.

How to Overcome
All Compulsive Behavior!

Most people on the spiritual path are obsessed with some compulsive behavior. It could involve drugs, alcohol, delicious food, romance, compulsive spending, etc. Meditation on the Emptiness of Time is the solution. Obsessions of the mind are hard to subdue. Will power is what most people use. And if will power was really a good answer, there would not be so many addiction programs available.

Do not despair. The emptiness of time meditation is the answer. All of these obsessions arise in the present which is not real. Once this is easily realized, any and all obsessions disappear as totally unreal. This is also true of greed, anger, depression, fear, guilt etc.

Owner's Manual For The Human Mind 76

The really hard part is getting this inferential realization the first time and getting it consistently. Once it's realized the first time, it must be cultivated daily, Then it's easy. Otherwise not so easy.

Understanding Ontology

Part 3

This section is totally necessary! Do not move on until you understand it perfectly!

All of the chapters in Nagarjuna's Fundamental Principles of the Middle Way prove that it's totally and logically impossible for cause and effect to be real. This opposes the testimony of our senses. We see cause and effect in operation everywhere, and we believe it's real based on the fact that we can actually rely on it to achieve our goals.

If we have a headache we take aspirin as cause, and a few minutes later we have the effect of our headache being gone. We itch as a cause, and our tickle is gone with a few scratches. We see the light turn red as a cause, and then we see traffic stop as an effect. We go to work as a cause, and we receive a deposit in our bank account as the effect of our being paid for our work. The swimmer wins a race as a cause, and we see him receive a trophy as an effect. So cause and effect is everywhere!

Then the philosophers tell us what we believe to be real is actually like an illusion. Ultimate Reality is not what we observe and think instinctively to be real. It's called *samskara* but it's not real. Instead what we think to be real is really like and illusion. Ultimate Reality can not be described inferentially because there is nothing like it in samskara to compare it to.

But Ultimate Reality can be realized in meditation inferentially at first. Most all of these realizations described throughout Fundamental Principles turn out to be very simple things. We think there are two things, but once analyzed they turn out to be a single thing. Or it turns out to be something we can't find.

We start first with cause and effect itself. Cause comes first and the effect comes second. We believe they are two different things, but they are not. Instead they are one (1) thing only.

We believe the perceiver and the object of perception are two different things. The object of perception comes first and the perceiver perceives it, But these are not two separate things. In fact they are actually the same thing.

And this is not the only mistake we make. Sometimes it's the other way around. In Understanding Ontology Part 1 we understood how we thought our body and it's parts were the same thing. But they are not. They are two different things. But when we searched for it, we did not find our own body where it's supposed to be: that is, outside in what we think is the real world. In fact we could not find our body at all. And since it exists, there is only one logical place for it to be – inside our own mind, like in a dream.

In Understanding Ontology Part 2, we could not find the present moment anywhere. And since it exists, the only logical place is inside our mind – not in the outside world.

How Is Emptiness Realized
Inferentially?

When we see smoke coming from a chimney, we inferentially realize there must be a fire inside. In fact we can rely on it. If we went into the house, we would be sure to directly see the fire. This is the inference.

In the same way, once we realize the Knowledge of emptiness inferentially, we can rely on the fact that we'll be able to realize it directly – the deeper we go in meditation.

The First (1st) Mahayana Path of Learning

Meditation is the easiest way to realize emptiness. This is done in a three (3) step process. The first thing we have to understand is the logic. If we understand the logic, we have progressed to the Mahayana Buddhist First Path of Learning. Congratulations! Welcome to the First Path of Learning.

The Mahayana Second (2nd) Path Of Learning

Owner's Manual For The Human Mind 79

Once we realize it inferentially, we will be able to demonstrate it in our own life. If we are sick, we can get will. If we are suffering emotionally we will be able to end all emotional pain immediately. So this is a very useful and practical thing to have during this lifetime, in between lifetimes, or even future lifetimes. When we can do this, we have been promoted to The Second (2ⁿᵈ) Mahayana Path of learning. Congratulations, we have progressed to the Mahayana Second (2ⁿᵈ) Path of Learning.

The Mahayana Third (3ʳᵈ) Path of Learning

This happens when we have a direct experience of emptiness. In this case if we are sick, we will be able to have instantaneous healings for many kinds of illnesses. In the writer's own experience, he was instantly healed of the Swine Flu.

There are two more Mahayana Paths of Learning – the Fourth (4ᵗʰ) and The Fifth (5ᵗʰ). However, these two Paths will not be discussed. This is because the writer can't actually demonstrate them. So why speculate. The reader is urged to find someone qualified to share his or her experience on these two Paths.

Actual Realization

The author describes it this way. Concentrating on Nagarjuna's logic deep in meditation is called, "Analytical Meditation." This is done from the point of what's called, "Calm abiding." In time from watching the breath, the mind will just sink deep into this state. There are two ways to reach it.

The fist way is to just watch the breath, with or without a mantra, until the mind sinks into a pleasurable state of bliss. Then when all sorts of thoughts enter the mind – like analytical meditation – the depth of meditation is not disturbed.

The second way to reach, "Calm abiding," is by taking the bull by the horns so to speak. By simply concentrating on the Nagarjuna's logic: that is, just rehashing it over and over in the mind, until he or she gets to calm abiding. This happens simply by normal concentration on a single subject – blocking out all thoughts not connected logically with the subject of meditation.

How long will it take to get there? With a little practice, we can get there almost at once. Sometimes it happens instantly. In fact that's what we try to do: that is, get there immediately. With me it works like this. I get there instantly most of the time. But many times I can not get there at all. Or when I do get there, the realization of emptiness is not very deep and doesn't take hold to end my suffering. Or I only get partial relief. Or I may have to struggle, struggle, struggle, etc.

I have a cousin who is an inventor. I've never talked to him about it, but I personally believe his inventions come from long hours of thinking through the problem again, again, again, etc. What I believe happens with inventors is the same thing that happens with me, the knowledge of emptiness arises. The knowledge of the solution for the inventor arises too.

In fact the knowledge of the solution to all problems and obstructions is emptiness. That of course may or may not help inventors. For me, this knowledge arises and is actually different from the logic that proceeds it. The knowledge and emptiness are the same thing. What is emptiness? It's Knowledge. The obstructions in life are seen for what they are: that is, knowledge only – emptiness only. For example, the knowledge of why anger is an illusion arises. This knowledge takes precedence over the testimony of our senses.

This is not a willful act of suppressing the testimony of our senses. It happens easily and spontaneously! The knowledge arises and the obstruction is gone. The obstruction melts into a space-like vacuity. But it's really because of the knowledge (same as emptiness) that arises. Until the Knowledge arises, the obstruction remains.

How the Author Demonstrates The Emptiness
OF Time In His Own Life

On method is to deal with illness. I'm 82-years-of-age and am plagued with little aches and pains. Or in many cases I get tired easily, and even though I get enough sleep, I get tired and it seems like I have to take an nap.

In meditation I try to visualize Nagarjuna's argument of coming and going. Since time comes and goes, according to Nagarjuna, it's empty of coming and going. But Everything that happens in samskara seemingly happens in the present. In the springtime with a great deal of rain or a good sprinkler system, we can almost see the grass grow.

In the morning the grass is mowed and within a short time, less than an hour, the manicured and very even lawn, is now infested with tiny blades or shoots of unevenness. If we check

Owner's Manual For The Human Mind 81

logically inside our own mind to see if this is real, we search all the
time that has passed and and all the time that is yet to pass.

We easily establish a past and we easily establish a future.
But where oh where is the present? There is actually no logical
present. No matter how much willpower we use to try to force a
logical opening between the past and future, the more we realize
the futility of finding the present. There is simply no place for
those shoots to arise if the world was real. Again and again we go
over and over the logic. Since we can almost see the grass actually
growing, this becomes a frustrating waste of time. No matter how
much we try to force it, it's just not logical that anything can grow
in the present. Logically it's not possible to find a present moment
anywhere between the past and future.

Finally the knowledge of emptiness arises. This knowledge
and emptiness are exactly the thing and the seemingly real world
melts into a space-like vacuity. It's seen for what it really is,
something like an illusion, like a dream – totally unreal. There is
no way to describe it inferentially because there are no words in
any language that are like it.

Back to my little aches and pains. No matter how hard we
look, there is no present. According to the testimony of our senses,
my little aches and pains arose in the present just like the grass.
There is no place for anything to arise any place else. I agree! I
hurt in the present! But where is the present? It's no place to be
found logically. Since I still hurt, I try to make a place for it. It's
frustrating.

The testimony of my senses tell me there is a present. So
I'm bound and determined to find it. But I can't and finally I just
give up. Then suddenly the knowledge of emptiness arises which is
exactly the same as emptiness itself. There's no way to describe it
because there are no words in any language to describe it.

For those who doubt Nagarjuna's logic and still believe an
inherently existing present moment exists, **I ask each and every
one of you, then why do my little aches and pains disappeared
each time?**

A few days ago, I woke up with a continuing illness. My
gums get infected from time to time. A few days ago, I woke up
with swollen gums and pain. Nothing serious but ti takes a few
weeks of special treatment.

Again back to analyzing to see if it's real or just another of *samskara's* illusion like appearances. Conventionally everything arises arises in the present. Therefore, if that's true, I will logically find the place where my swollen gums arose. But I can't. It's so frustrating because I hurt. And if that hurt is real, I should be able to find where it arises. As long as it has arisen, it must have only arisen in this present moment which I can't find.

So I go back to trying to find it somewhere between the past and future. But I still can't. Finally my mind accepts Nagarjuna's logic and my the bad gums and pain disappear inside my mind. It's replaced by a knowledge that's the same as emptiness. And I dwell in suchness and bliss as much as possible throughout the day.

When the meditation is over, I go back to believing the bad gums and emptiness are real. So my gums are still swollen and it still hurts. But I also know that an inferential realization will hasten the healing process considerably. A direct experience may cure it instantly. And an inferential realization will heal it much faster, so I concentrate on those thoughts the rest of the day.

For those who doubt Nagarjuna's logic and still believe a present moment actually inherently exists, **I ask each and every one of you, then why did most of the swelling go down on my gums within an hour and both swelling and pain disappear by the end of the day? I did nothing else for healing.**

This is because emptiness is not only a scientific philosophy. It's also a scientific process that can be demonstrated. And since I developed this ability to demonstrate it's effectiveness in a few days or weeks once I understood it, I believe anyone can demonstrate emptiness in his or her life just as fast or even sooner. Because it is so very simple, realizing the knowledge of emptiness can't be something that even takes three months. A few days or weeks should be plenty. Most should find this Knowledge long before three (3) months.

Based on the above reasoning, the commentaries on each of the chapters of Nagarjuna's Fundamental Principals that follow will be explained with as little commentary as possible. If you are having trouble realizing emptiness inferentially, it's suggested, go back to Understanding Ontology Parts 1,2, &3.

Do Not Despair!

Yes, it,s frustrating at firsts. "First Things First!" The very first thing is NOT realizing emptiness inferentially. The very first thing is to get to The First (1st) Mahayana Path. All that's required in the beginning is to just understand the logic. As long as a person can understand Nagarjuna's logic, then he or she is absolutely guaranteed to progress to the Second (2nd) Mahayana Path which will automatically permit demonstration. Once this happens, killing all emotional pain immediately will happen easily. We will not only understand emptiness, but we will also demonstrate it in our lives by killing all emotional pain immediately and more.

In this section we've mentioned little aches and pains, depression and some others. However all suffering can be pacified. This includes all the emotional feelings like anger, greed, fear, depression, guilt, etc. It will also work for all physical pain too – not only the little aches and pains of some old guy like me.

Chapter 1

Fundamental Principals OF
The Middle Way
Commentary

An Examination of
Causal Conditions

Nagarjuna's Salutation
In The Beginning:

I Prostrate To The One
Who Teaches That Whatever
Is Dependently Arisen
Does Not Arise
Does Not Cease
Is Not Permanent
Does Not Come
Does Not Go
Is Neither One Thing
Nor Different Things
I Prostate To The Perfect Buddha
The Supreme Of All Who Speak
Who Completely Dissolves All Fabrications
And Teaches Peace

Thus we learn from the start, there are eight (8) aspects to emptiness.

1, Anything dependently arisen.
2, Does not arise.
3, Does not cease.
4, Is Not Permanent
5, Does not Come
6, Does not go.
7, Is not one thing.
8, Is not different things.

Because of these, in the *Madhyamaka* tradition emptiness is defined as anything dependently arisen.

Here Nagarjuna uses a tetra-lemma, same as the Greeks. It consists of four (4) arguments. If any single argument is true, it would prove inherent reality: that is, *samskara* is real. If none of them are true, it proves that samskara is a total illusion, empty of inherent existence. The four (4) arguments cover all the bases for inherent reality to exist.

NO fifth (5th) argument for inherent reality exists.

First (1st) argument: Things arise in the universe of themselves.

Second (2nd) argument: Things arise because of some other.

Third (3rd) argument: Things arise because of themselves and another.

Fourth (4th) and last argument: NOT without causes and conditions.

Please note: there is no fifth (5th) argument possible!

Madhyamaka proves that all four of the above arguments are impossible logically. Therefore, the world as we know it can't be inherently real. That is, nothing can exist from it's own side (outside in the seemingly real world). Instead it only exists inside our own minds.

We will tackle all of the above arguments very briefly. If the arguments in the first chapter were all that there were, it might not be convincing. But these arguments combined with the remaining chapters provide overwhelming proof.

Chapter 1 contains all the philosophy and logic for the

entire Buddhist School of *Madhyamaka*. This is beyond the scope of this commentary, which only emphasizes killing all emotional pain immediately and not necessarily the entire in depth intricacies of enlightenment. Most of the remaining chapters are not so complex. They are all so very simple that they can be explained in just a page or two (2).

Argument 1, if things arose of themselves, they would have to already exist. And what need would there be to arise the second time in the seemingly real world? And if they did arise by themselves, what would there be to stop them from arising again and again – totally uncontrolled? And if things arose of themselves, why aren't extinct species like the dinosaurs being replaced?

Argument 2: Things arise from another. This is mainly directed against God. If things did arise from God, this is illogical. That is, who made God? And if God did create it all, why did God create it? The obvious answer is because of desire. And since desire is considered ontologically unreal which will be explained in other chapters, such a God could NOT be supreme. That is, God would suffer because of his or her desires and operate on the same level as ignorant humans who also suffer because of their desires. Could such a god be supreme?

Argument 3: things arise from themselves and another (God) also fails. If argument 1 and 2 fail, it's logically impossible for their combination to cause anything to arise.

Argument 4: NOT without causes and conditions. This seems like it's the only logical way for anything to arise. We have all of newton's laws of motion that imply the laws of cause and affect are real. However, the law of cause and affect is totally unreal. If things did rise because of cause and affect, they would have to follow a sequence: that is, the cause must precede the affect. But in fact, cause and affect can not happen sequentially or simultaneously.

We have a volatile substance and a spark. Which comes first, the spark or the explosion? The professor and most of us say, "The spark." But the spark is not a cause. It's a potential cause but not a cause. By definition, the spark can only be a cause after the explosion has taken place. At first this seem difficult to understand. The following analogy, owever, should make it crystal clear.

Which comes first today in the Twenty First Century, the father or the son? The biologist says, "The father." But as stated before, a father can't be a father until first there is a son. To say the son comes first is totally ridiculous. How can that be cause and affect? Supposing we say the father and son come together simultaneously. This is not cause and affect either. Coming together simultaneously is what happens with two horns of a bull – neither horn has any apparent affect upon the other.

Therefore, cause and affect can NOT happen sequentially and they can NOT happen simultaneously. If it were possible to actually construct an inherently real world with real volatile substances like gunpowder and sparks, a unique question arises?

Could an explosion, that was actually real, take place? As defined, the sparks are not causes and can never be causes. This is because for them to be causes, they must have already caused the explosion. If a real spark (a real potential cause) came in contact with real gunpowder, would this real potential cause then mysteriously change into a real cause? And if so, would there be an explosion?

There is controversy in thought. In order for something to be real, it can't change. So could real gunpowder and real potential cause result in an explosion? According to some, the explosion could not take place. But in unreal *samskara* an explosion is no problem.

Yet we can't say causes and conditions don't exist. Only that they don't exist based upon cause and affect. And we can not say that things do not arise from causes and condition. But the results are only appearances. We call this appearance emptiness.

A tree seed with the conditions of soil, moisture, etc. does transform into a tree. But the tree is not real. It looks real and the rest of our senses tell us it's real. But it's not. It's only appearance emptiness. The tree, the soil, the moisture and everything else is only appearance emptiness – unreal – like something arising in a dream. We proved the tree unreal in Understanding Ontology, Part 1.

Finally with trees and everything else there must be a primary cause. And if we search back, we find that a tree requires a seed to become a tree, but we need a tree to produce a seed. And so we have an infinite regression when we try to trace it back to the first seed or the first tree. A primary causes in our seemingly real world can NOT be found.

Ultimately *Madhyamaka* comes to the conclusion that all of *samskara* existed from beginning-less time. They not only reject the idea that God created it, they reject the idea that anyone created it. *Samskara* just appears and changes due to causes and conditions. It has always done it this way and it always will.

This is because anything that is beginningless is also endless. As long as it's not as creator of *samskara*, there is no objection to God or that God is beginningless, but in that case God would be unreal – appearance emptiness also. We too according to *Madhyamaka* are beginningless which means we are endless. At the same time, we too are unreal, existing like a dream.

When we become enlightened, we become omniscient. Neither *Madhyamaka* nor Vedanta claim we become omnipotent – all powerful. But due to the nature of samskara, being omniscient automatically means we are omnipotent – all powerful. But this is never claimed.

Chapter 1 involving these four (4) arguments of the tetra-lemma have been addressed superficially on purpose. If we look at comparative arguments from Advaita Vedanta and others we get into a great deal of controversy. For example, Advaita Vedanta seems to contradict *Madhyamaka* by stating only God is real – everything else is unreal. Noting is real in *Madhyamaka,* and that includes God, too.

Vedanta claims we have a soul or *autman* (Sanskrit). *Madhyamaka* says we have a continuum but it's not like a soul. Ultimately the individual soul or *autman (*Sanskrit) in Vedanta is believed to be God or Brahman, totally in contradiction to Chapter 1 and many other perspectives.

But there are similarities. Both are monists: that is, the final realization is that the observer is none other than the observation.

Madhyamaka asserts Samskara and Emptiness are the same entity. Vedanta's Mundukya Upanishad says the same thing.

Both claim the only creator is ignorance. Ignorance is not from beginningless time. If that were the case, ignorance would also be endless. Nobody could acquire wisdom.

And similarly, wisdom doesn't exist from beginningless time. Otherwise, ignorance would not be possible.

And even without comparing *Madhyamaka* to Advaita Vedanta, we are burdened with some outlandish claims and assertions So those who study this first chapter should not make any rash judgments – all of which are NOT necessary for killing all emotional pain immediately.

Now that this first chapter is out of the way, both Advaita Vedanta and *Madhyamaka* are totally compatible with most of the logic and reason in the following chapters. This is also true of any other philosophy or religion as well.

The newcomer to this philosophy will find the remaining chapters simple, easy, and enjoyable to understand. Additionally each of the following chapters will focus on killing all emotional pain immediately – NOT on enlightenment itself or religious dogma which would otherwise create controversy.

Teaching emptiness from the standpoint of actually killing all emotional suffering now makes it a useful and exciting adventure. Otherwise teaching emptiness or the science of Brahman from the standpoint of enlightenment becomes a useless mind game until one is enlightened of course. What good is it to teach all about emptiness or the science of Brahman if none of it can be demonstrated for years and years or even lifetimes?

The aim of this book is to teach emptiness or the science of Brahman in a few days or weeks – NOT more than (3) months: that is, how to actually kill all emotional pain immediately.

Chapter 2

Fundamental Principals OF
The Middle Way
Commentary

An Examination of
Coming and Going

We learned from Nagarjuna's opening salutation, there are eight (8) cardinal ways to identify emptiness: Chapter 2 deals with coming and going.

Samskara can be categorized into it's constituents or aggregates. There are five of them which are:

> 1, Form
> 2, Feelings
> 3, Perceptions
> 4, Mental activity
> 5, Consciousness

Can we guess which aggregate deals with suffering? It's Feelings. All suffering can be broken down into it's source: that is, Feelings. When we feel bad, we either feel bad emotionally or physically. There is no other way we can suffer. This is just common sense. It's necessary for us to take a moment to review our life experience. We must ask ourselves, Is there any other way we can suffer? The answer is an emphatic, "No!"

And from our own experience, we know suffering comes and goes which are two (2) of the cardinal identifiers of emptiness. So we know right off the bat, all suffering is emptiness, unreal, like a dream. And if we took a test on Nagarjuna's book, we could easily answer the question correctly, Is coming and going empty of inherent existence? Our answer is, "Yes!"

But would this end our suffering? Unless we realize this fact while we are suffering, we are not going to end our suffering. Additionally we may have already realized it some time ago. But now our same suffering is back. Unless we realize it again during the time of this suffering, it will also not kill our suffering.

Anytime suffering arises, if we expect to kill our suffering immediately, we will have to realize emptiness of coming and going as one method. Naturally there are many more ontological methods. Eventually our realizations will become steady. In this case suffering will not arise. Neither physical nor emotional suffering can arise when our realization of coming and going is steady.

The cure involves replacing the testimony of our senses that feels pain with the logic and reason of our intellect – telling us all coming and going is unreal.

Assume we are are suffering with depression. Nagarjuna's logic that coming and going is unreal, empty, and like a dream is simply this. Let's look at our depression. Where has it come from and where is it going?

1, We find a place for all the depression that has passed.

2, And we find a place for all the depression that is about to pass.

3, But we can find no logical place for any depression to cause pain now in the present.

On the path that has been traveled, we find no pain because it already happened and is like water that flowed under the bridge – gone! And on the future path, we find no pain. This is only common sense and reason. The pain on the path we already traveled is over. The future path hasn't happened yet.

Between these two paths there is no place for pain to be found in the middle – the present moment. We have completely covered our paths. Depression pain has no place to be found now – in the present. There's just no place for it. Also nowhere can we find movement. But if there's no place for depression to happen in the present, why am I in pain now?

This leaves us with one conclusion, the pain we are experiencing now must be an illusion, unreal like a dream. Yes depression hurts. The cure in meditation involves replacing the pain from the testimony of the our senses with the logic of our intellect – telling us our depression has no place to be found.

The pain we are experiencing is only appearance emptiness. And when we realize this, our depression is gone. Where did it go? Where did it come from? Replacing the pain from depression is a space like vacuity representing an inferential realization of emptiness has taken place. In place of the pain the knowledge of emptiness exists. And as long as we have this realization, no emotional pain will ever arise – ever!

Supposing events happen that would normally make us angry, fearful, greedy, jealous, or whatever. These emotions along with all others will not arise: that is, as long as our realization of the emptiness of time is happening. Otherwise it's back to the emotional pain again.

Physical Healing

Supposing we have a headache. We search for this headache everywhere. Where did it come from? We search the path of our coming and going. On all the path we have already traveled, we find no headache pain. All of this pain has already happened there.

And on the path we intend to go, we find no headache pain either. That's because the pain has not happened there yet. Logically we find no place the headache pain to exist now. Then why do we have headache pain now?

The answer is simple. Our head pain is empty of coming and going. It's an illusion, unreal, like a dream. The cure involves replacing the headache pain from the testimony of our senses with the wisdom of our intellect: that is, wisdom of emptiness. By meditating this way, the mind falls into a space like vacuity. When this happens, we have just realized the emptiness of time inferentially and the pain from our headache is gone immediately. Replacing it is the knowledge of emptiness.

Even though we have not realized emptiness directly, the pain from our headache is gone. More serious illness doesn't end so immediately. But based on our own personal experience, we will find healing will happen very quickly if we have treated all physical illness this way.

Based on the testimony of the author's experience, a direct Samadhi experience of emptiness killed his swine flu immediately. Therefore, it is possible to kill all illness in the same simple way. A simple inferential realization of emptiness – even though not a direct realization – will cure a simple headache. And even if it's

NOT cured, the inferential realization will hasten healing. This happens even though there is no desire for it to happen. That's because we discover all emotional and physical pain is an illusion, unreal, like a dream – unable to really hurt us.

There is an advantage to healing this way. There are other methods of healing that will cure illness too. They have to do with having faith that God will heal us, or using will power to employ positive thought as with Raja Yoga, etc. All these other methods heal too, but at the same time they may increase our selfishness and self-centeredness for worldly ambition towards health and vitality. That is, they foster and enforce our egotistical desire for health.

Desire and aversion is the defect that causes *samskara* to perpetuate. Killing emotional pain with emptiness does not foster our desires. Instead it fosters a proper view of Ultimate Reality – that nothing is real.

There are only two ways we can be going – toward enlightenment or away from it. By using emptiness to treat both emotional illness and physical illness, we are going toward our goal. This is because meditation on emptiness kills our selfishness and self-centeredness which is the real obstruction to renunciation of all worldly ambitions – including health and vitality.

In fact during the meditation on emptiness there is no thoughts of getting well – only that the illness is an illusion, unreal, empty, like a dream etc. The cure involves knowing the mental affliction is unreal and can NOT hurt us. Enlightenment involves knowing the same thing. Therefore we are going toward enlightenment and this happens if we know or don't know anything about enlightenment.

It could be argued, as long as selfish desire is an obstruction, then why bother to realize emptiness and kill all pain? This is because desire is required to realize emptiness.

This is not a valid argument. That would be like saying, when our hand is being burned by a hot stove, why remove it? In the same way when we are being burned by the illusion like *samskara*, it's simply logical to remove the pain. It's only common sense to practice the mental logic of Ultimate Reality: that is, to see things as they really are rather than as they appear to be. It's total insanity to suffer aimlessly in *samskara* and not desire to realize emptiness, which is the greatest of healers too.

Chapter 3

Fundamental Principals OF
The Middle Way
Commentary

An Examination Of
The Source Of Consciousness

Samskara can be categorized by it's constituents or aggregates. There are five of them which are:

> 1, Form
> 2, Feelings
> 3, Perceptions
> 4, Mental activity
> 5, Consciousness

Chapter 3 also deals with the aggregate of perceptions. If our perceptions are appearance emptiness, then no emotional pain perceived can be real. This includes feelings.

Nagarjuna wrote this chapter for people who said, "Things are real because we perceive them." It addresses consciousness – our inner and outer awareness of our senses: that is, eyes, ears, feelings, smell, taste and mind. There are 6 inner sources and there are 6 outer sources. For example there is the eye that sees the perceived object and the self who perceives it.

The Heart Sutra tells us that all 6 sources of consciousness – inner and outer that equal 12 – are empty, unreal, like a dream.

Those people opposed to this teaching saw a flower and said, "Because the eye sees a flower, the eye must be real." Nagarjuna did not believe the eye saw at all. He argued, "If the eye can't even see itself, how can it be real?"

Before medical science explained all the intricacies of how the eye works, it was harder to prove emptiness. Now it's actually easier to prove logically. If the eye were real, Nagarjuna says, perception would have to follow an orderly sequence of cause and affect. In that case:

What comes first, the inner source of consciousness, the perceiver (the self), or the perceived object (the flower)? According to medical science (biology), an image is reflected in the eye which is somehow transmitted to the brain. The brain is what we might call the self or perceiver today.

Only trouble is a real perceiver and a real object of perception do not exist alone – all by themselves – individually. Instead of being two things, they are actually one. This is because a real object of perception can only be an object of perception if there's something perceiving it. And vice versa is also true. A perceiver can't be real unless it perceives something.

Therefore a real perceiver and object of perception can not come together by cause and affect because neither can exist initially to come together sequentially or simultaneously. This makes no difference if there is or there is not a lag in contact due to the electrical charge that supposedly takes place before they come together. The lag in contact is all part of the illusion like appearance.

The real issue is actual existence before the supposed contact. Neither can exist alone, so how can they ever come together. In order to come together, if the are real, they must first exist which they can not do.

The illusion is that they can exist all alone by themselves. In emptiness we perceive them together as one thing. But we write this, The perceiver's object of perception. The ("'s") signifies that the perceiver possesses the object, In that case, they must be different things. The possessor must be different than the possesse. But how can they be two things that come together in cause and affect. Neither can come together. Neither can exist by itself.

Inner And Outer Sources Of Feelings

Instead of the world being real, *Madhyamaka* asserts that *samskara* is imputed upon our minds something like a dream. If the world were actually real, nothing could be called a perceiver without there being an object of perception – already stated.

But the world is not real and we take for granted our illogical cause and affect universe. Even more perplexing is that we know we are in a constant state of change. This alone suggests nothing is real, but we never view the world as even slightly unreal. When we are happy, we consider that happiness is real, that we have always been happy and, therefore, we will always be happy.

A few minutes later we're depressed, and we think we've always been depressed, and we'll always be depressed. Anything real never changes. And we think our depression is real.
In fact if depression were real, we'd would actually always be depressed, and it would never change. Likewise, if we were angry, and anger were real, we would always be angry.

So it's time to questions our feelings, especially painful feelings like greed, anger, fear, depression and guilt. One of the best ways of doing that is by using Nagarjuna's reasoning: that is, that perception could never have arisen in the first place based upon cause and affect.

After the depressed self (perceiver) arises with the object of perception (emotional pain), there is a simple meditation cure. It involves simply replacing the testimony of the 12 inner and outer sources of consciousness with the wisdom of our intellect.

We ask ourselves, which came first, the depressed perceiver (depressed self) or the object of perception (the Pain)? And because they can't exist alone, neither can exist to actually come fist. So right off the bat a depression can't be real. Logic already stated above.

Our subtler minds will accept this logic, and when this happens, our depression will dissolve into a space-like vacuity and be gone immediately. When the knowledge of emptiness arises, the pain disappears.

Depression as well all the mental afflictions do arise, but they can't arise by cause and effect. The only logical reason they exist is because they were imputed, like a dream is imputed – all at once. The perceiver and perceived object must, therefore, be imputed together. This is because they can't exist alone to actually come together.

  In the next chapter, Chapter 4, Nagarjuna tackles the aspects of aggregates. This chapter covers why perceptions are not real based upon the perceiver and the object of perception never being able to come together through cause and effect. The next chapter deals with this same issue but gives another reason for emotional pain not being real. The reason is because a real cause can't be a real cause without causing something.

Chapter 4

Fundamental Principals OF
The Middle Way
Commentary

An Examination Of
The Aggregates

Samskara can be categorized by it's constituents or aggregates. There are five of them which are: 1 Form, 2 Feelings 3 Perceptions, 4 Mental activity, and 5 Consciousness

This chapter is similar to the last on. In this chapter Nagarjuna proves cause and affect aren't real because a real cause can not exist alone all by itself without a real affect? How can there be a cause without a corresponding affect. Or how can there be an affect without an corresponding cause? The logic is the same as Chapter 4.

It was given before, but which comes first today – not from ancient times but today in the modern world – the father or the son? It's not possible to be a father before there is a son. The son must come first in order for the father to even be a father. Yes this is ridiculous.

Which comes first, the spark that caused the explosion or the explosion itself? In order for the spark to the the spark that caused the explosion, the explosion must already have happened. So if we answered the father or the spark, we were wrong.

There are 6 inner sources and there are 6 outer sources. For example there is the eye and the perception of what we see. And this is true for all 6 sources of consciousness. Nagarjuna breaks it down to a perceiver and a perceived object.

The Heart Sutra tells us that all 6 sources of consciousness are empty, unreal, like a dream.

In this chapter Nagarjuna proves with sound reasoning that form doesn't really exist in his original commentary. But this doesn't help us with emotional pain. Therefore, we will concentrate on those aspects where we can kill all emotional pain immediately.

Nevertheless Nagarjuna's arguments of why form is not real holds true when it comes to feelings. If feelings were real, they would have to follow a logical sequence of cause and affect. Our object of perception (emotional pain as a cause) would have to come first and the perceiver (the hurting self would be the effect) would have to come second.

But this can't happen. This is because the object of pain is not a cause. It causes nothing without an effect. It only becomes a cause after we experience the effect – the painful self. If the world were actually real, this could never happen as it does in *samskara*. Yes, we do have pain. This is because of our unreal universe: that is, *samskara* is imputed conceptually upon our minds. It never happens through cause and affect which would be impossible if the world were actually real.

Inner And Outer Sources Of Feelings
Ending All Emotional Pain!

In Chapter 3 Nagarjuna used the fact that a real object of perception can not arise without a perceiver. Therefore, cause and effect can not come about sequentially or simultaneously.

In this Chapter 4, Nagarjuna proves with logical reasoning that a real cause can not ever arise – all alone – by itself. If it did, what would it cause? Therefore, cause and effect can not come about sequentially or simultaneously as it appears with cause and effect. Yes emotional pain exists but it's only appearance emptiness – nothing real, like an illusion, like a dream.

The very same thing is true about physical pain but it takes longer and is much harder to realize. Ending all emotional pain comes easily by understanding just a few of Nagarjuna's reasonings – even more easily when all of them are understood. This should be understood in a few days or weeks – NOT more than three months.

How to kill all emotional and physical pain is a really practical thing to know. We will be able to use this ability many times in our lifetime. Why not prepare now? There are national catastrophes, like fires, floods, earthquakes, snow storms, etc. And there is always the threat to catastrophic illness. These all pose the possibility of unbearable pain which could last for hours, days, weeks, months or even years.

Even more importantly, is how to cure even mild emotional pain like boredom, and the dullness of repetitive work. All of us are forced into pain from doing things we have to do, even if we don't want to do them. Meditation is a great example.

Doing long periods of meditation is painful. Yes, we have to go beyond this pain if we ever wish to be enlightened. How shall we do this? Through self-discipline? That is a possibility. But meditation is the easiest way is to understand all pain as an illusion, empty, unreal, like a dream. In this case the pain melts into a space-like like vacuity and it's gone. At the exact same time, the Knowledge of emptiness arises as the pain disappears.

Using the above method is much easier than suffering through the pain of self-discipline until the pain eventually disappears.

Caution: long periods of meditation can cause pain in our physical bodies – especially the knees – if we use the lotus posture. Long hours of just bearing the pain is not perhaps a good idea. This is because this has caused damage to the knees. Therefore, common sense and reason should be used also. When it comes to boredom, using emptiness to cure it can't be harmful. But it depends on the after affect. In any case, long hours of enduring any kind of pain – physical or emotional – is probably not a good idea.

In my own case, I endured pain for only about 15 minutes. Many times I threw in the towel before the 15 minutes were up.

Do Not Be Discouraged!

Once all the meditations are learned it will be easier. All that's necessary now is to enter the the First Level of Learning. As long as we understand the logical arguments, we are on the First Path, Once we do this, we will eventually enter the second path which involves an actual (inferential) realization. Therefore, as long as we understand the meditation, we are progressing. Once we've learned all the arguments, and even before this happens, we're guarantee that realization must come. That is, the mind (including all the pain) will melt into this space-like vacuity as the knowledge of emptiness arises.

Chapter 5

Fundamental Principals OF
The Middle Way
Commentary

An Examination Of
The Elements

Chapter 5 deals with the elements! We usually think of these today in terms of physics tables of the elements. During Nagarjuna's times, there wcre only 5 of them: that is, consciousness, space, water, fire, and earth. Nagarjuna's Fundamental Principles only deals with these. Consciousness is not an element however, because it can be broker down further as follows:

1, Eye consciousness
2, ear consciousness
3, feeling consciousness
4, taste consciousness.
5, smell consciousness

And feeling consciousness can be broken down into it's emotional elements which are:

1, Greed consciousness
2, Anger Consciousness
3, Fear Consciousness
4, Depression Consciousness
5, Guilt Consciousness

And all of the above categories can be broken down to it's final element. See Sublimation 1, for a full range of emotional elements. Using any method to describe our emotional pain, it becomes an actual element of consciousness. Let's assume it's jealousy. This as well as all other named emotional pains can not be broken down further.

According to Nagarjuna, all elements include two things. First (1ˢᵗ) there is the element itself, and second (2ⁿᵈ) there are the identifying characteristics.

In physics, for example, we first (1ˢᵗ) have an elements like gold and secondly (2ⁿᵈ) we have it's identifying characteristics (it's atomic weight etc.).

Whatever emotional pain we describe is that element of consciousness. It too is described the same way as in physics. First (1ˢᵗ) we have, for example, the conscious element jealousy, and secondly (2ⁿᵈ) we have the identifying characteristics (the intensity and kind of jealously).

If these elements are real, argues Nagarjuna, which came first in their order of cause and effect? Did the element come first (the jealousy)? Or did the identifying characteristics? (The intensity of our jealously or what kind of Jealously. For example mostly jealousy is based on greed. Other jealousy is based in hopeless depression or anger.)

Neither can come first. In fact they can't logically come together in a real world by cause and effect. This is because none of them can exist – all alone – by itself. How can there be a real element without a real identifying characteristic? How can there be an identifying characteristic without an element? So neither can exist all alone and come first. In fact none of the elements with their identifying characteristics can come together sequentially or simultaneously in a real world. However, our system of *samskara* that's unreal, like a dream easily accomplishes the task.

One might argue that the element and the identifying characteristic are the same entity. That is, the atomic weight of gold and gold itself are the same entity. But this is not the case. We write it, gold's atomic weight. The apostrophe, "s," signifies that gold possesses it's atomic weight. Therefore, the gold and atomic weight are different, because a possesse and a possessor must be different.

The cure is to realize all elements of emotional pain are unreal, like a dream. This is accomplished in meditation by concentrating on the ontological arguments. Finally the wisdom of emptiness arises. This starves out the illusion of the testimony of our unreal senses. When this happens, our jealousy will dissolve into a space-like vacuity. And jealously or any other emotional pain will be gone.

Ending Physical Pain

All physical pain is unreal, like an illusion, like a dream. This is realized with the same meditation, The physical pain can't come first. That's because no pain can exist anywhere without identifying characteristics. The identifying characteristics of pain are where the pain is located and what kind. Tingling is pain. Is there sharp tingling? Or dull tinging?

Therefore, physical pain can't come together sequentially or simultaneously with it's identifying characteristics by cause and affect in our seemingly real world. This is because it can't exist by itself to actually come first. However, our unreal world of samskara easily accomplishes the task by imputing the physical pain on our minds like dream pain.

Instead of taking aspirin every time we have a headache, why not practice by dissolving the unreal pain into a space-like vacuity using the above meditation.

Forcing Ourselves To Do Meditation!

Instead of using willpower to endure the pain of forcing ourselves to sit in meditation, why not practice by dissolving the unreal pain (physical or emotional) into a space-like vacuity and cure it? Caution: long periods of voluntarily enduring any pain for more than 15 minutes probably is not a good idea. This is especially true of physical pain.

Chapter 6

Fundamental Principals OF
The Middle Way
Commentary

An Examination of Desire
&
The Desirous One

Samskara can be categorized by it's constituents or aggregates. There are five of them which are:

1, Form
2, Feelings
3, Perceptions
4, Mental activity
5, Consciousness

Chapter 6 deals with desire. It is generally believed that desire defiles us. However, in this chapter Nagarjuna makes the point that desire is pure. We have angry desires that wish to inflict harm and even death on those around us. How about these desires? Surely these defile us? But Nagarjuna says, "No!"

Desires like these and or sexual impropriety are all pure, and are NOT different than those desires in a dream. If desire was real, it would have to arise due to cause and affect. In that case desire would have to arise sequentially or simultaneously. Desire never arises without a desirous one.

How can desire arise first? There has never been a desire

without a desirous one. How can the desirous one come first? There has never been a desirous one without a desire. And for them to come together simultaneously, desire and the desirous one would first have to arise individually – all alone – by themselves. And since they can"t do that, it's impossible for them to come together sequentially or simultaneously due to cause and effect.

If desire could arise without a desirous one, then dependent on that, desire would be real. If a desirous one could arise without a desire, then dependent on that, the desirous one would be real.

Once the wisdom of our intellect grasps this, we understand that desire and the desirous one are imputed together upon our minds. Both the desire and the desirous one are illusions, unreal, like a dream.

This wisdom permits us to see that our continuum – the observer – exists in a different realm than the unreal dream states. When the desire and the desirous one melt into a space-like vacuity, it's like being in an impregnable fortress. What arises along with the Knowledge of emptiness is the knowledge that fires can not burn me, winds can't dry me, weapons can't cut me, and disease can't touch me.

Devotees on the spiritual path usually have problems with intoxicants, compulsive spending, overeating or some obsession with excessive desire that causes pain and suffering. Indeed if we use will power to suppress any desire, the result will be some kind of emotional pain depending on our past karma. It will either cause anger, frustration, fear depression or guilt. Obsession with food of course is greed. And many including this author has suffered long and agonizing emotional pain and grief because of compulsive overeating.

However, realizing that the unreal desire to compulsively overeat always arises with the one who desires to compulsively overeat and is imputed upon the mind the same way a dream is imputed, makes control easy and simple. The old saying is that sticks and stones can break my bones, but words will never hurt me.

This realization is that sticks and stones might break my bones, but desire is unreal and can never affect me.

Note: the Buddha taught the law of karma. So how can Nagarjuna say that desire can never harm us? If we are enlightened, the law of karma can't harm us. In the case of Buddhas, all thoughts are pure including desire. In a later chapter,

Nagarjuna proves the law of karma is unreal with sound reasoning. Otherwise in this unreal world, anger the worst of all mental defilements will impair us with karmic debt.

Do we have to undergo all the negative karma we've accumulated? According to Nagarjuna, we can escape all Karmic debt. According to him, it's all unreal so we escape by realizing it. That's Nagarjuna's point with desire, for Buddhas desire including all impure thoughts are pure, because it's like they never happened. If it never happened, then how can it be anything at all.

This is not some kind of Metaphysical Truth to be taken on blind faith. This can actually be demonstrated. How? By destroying all these obsessions of the mind any time they arise. When any of these obsessive desires arise and are pacified by wisdom, we have proof. We have just escaped karmic debt.

Chapter 7

Fundamental Principals OF
The Middle Way
Commentary

An Examination
Of The Composite

According to *Madhyamaka*, nothing has an essence of it's own. Everything that arises requires causes and conditions. Upon our arising, there was the condition requiring we have a father and mother. Our abiding requires that we first arise. And for us to cease, it requires arising and abiding. Once we analyze all the causes and conditions involved, we can clearly understand we have no essence at all. And neither does anything else.

Nagarjuna comments on this by telling us, "It's like we never existed." It's like we were never born. It's like we never abided and it's like we never died – all like a dream.

If we were truly real, we would exist on our own without causes and conditions. And we could abide on our own without causes and conditions – something that could exist completely on it's own. Arising would not depend on conditions. Abiding would not depend on conditions. And ceasing would not depend abiding or arising. If that were the case, we could declare we are inherently real.

Therefore arising, abiding and ceasing aren't real. This is because all of these events require causes and conditions. Even if we did not need parents to arise, we would still need causes and conditions. The first condition being that we were not already arisen. Or if we were already arisen, we would have to cease in order to arise. In order to abide, we would have to arise. And in order to cease we need to arise and abide first. So neither arising, abiding or ceasing can be inherently real. They all require causes and conditions.

It's like we were born in a dream, we got sick with a deathly disease. Just before we died, we woke up. Would that dream character ever die?

Not unless we went back to that dream. But supposing we didn't wake up? Could we ever die?

Supposing we died in the dream, would we be dead? Of course not!

Supposing we died in this unreal world of *samskara,* would we be dead? How could we ever die if we have actually never been born?

Arising, abiding and ceasing is what happens with all emotional pain. Yes, anger arises because of causes and conditions. We have been insulted and we are angry. And we desire revenge! But why should we want revenge if the anger itself never arose, doesn't abide now, and will never cease later?

We are depressed and we want to kill ourselves in a dream. Once we wake up, we realize the depression never really happened, abided nor ceased. We are depressed in this seemingly real life and we want to kill ourselves. Why should we kill ourselves? Like in the dream, depression never arose, abided or ceased in what we mistakenly think is real life.

Once the wisdom of our intellect understands this and rules over the testimony of the senses, our depression as well as any other emotional pain will dissolve in a space-like vacuity and be gone immediately. At exactly the exact same time the Knowledge of emptiness arises along with the bliss of prajana.

Therefore, things that arise, abide and cease do really exist but are only appearance – appearance emptiness – not anything real!

Chapter 8

Fundamental Principals OF
The Middle Way
Commentary

An Examination Of
Actors and Actions

Nagarjuna composed this chapter because of people who believed that composite things exist inherently. Someone builds a wagon, for example. According to them, because we experience the wagon with our senses, it exists inherently. But actors and actions can not come about through real cause and affect. It is only appearance emptiness.

If actors and actions actually took place and were inherently real, one of them would have to come first. Or they might come together simultaneously. But they can't actually do that. This is because neither actors nor actions can exist – independently – all alone – by themselves.

There is not one single action anywhere in samskara without an actor. And there is not one single actor in the world anywhere that can exist without an action. So they can't come together by cause and effect. In order to do that actors would have to exist by themselves – all alone – individually which they can't do.

Instead they are imputed upon our minds together, the same way it happens in dreams. Instead of actual cause and effect, we have causes and conditions coming together in dream appearance only. It's appearance only – appearance emptiness – totally unreal.

Someone insults us. Is the insult inherently real. We have the action of the insult. And we have the person (actor) who insulted us. Anger arises within us. Is this anger inherently real? We are the insulted actor, taking the action of seeking revenge. We believe our anger is real. We think here is real cause and affect.

We therefore, feel justified in taking the action of ill-will (anger). But neither we, our angry-self, (the actor) nor the ill-will (action) actually exist inherently. Both are imputed upon our minds together because of unreal causes and conditions. This is only common sense and reason. Neither the angry self (actor) not the ill will (action) can exist independently – all alone – by itself. They can, therefore, neither come together sequentially nor simultaneously in real cause and effect.

But are they a single entity? We write this, "The angry self's (actor's) ill will (action). The, "'s," signifies possession. This means the angry self (actor) owns or possesses the ill-will. This makes them different entities because the possessor must be different than the possesse. But if they were different, they could stand alone which they can't. Noting real could exist inherently like this. Therefore they must be unreal.

All emotional pain can be analyzed this way. All emotional pain involves an actor and action. We, the actor, our miserable-self feels justified in taking the action of dwelling in misery. The miserable-self (actor) and the misery (action) actually arise together. They are not cause and effect at all. Common sense says, they are imputed on our minds, and therefore, appearance only – appearance emptiness – totally unreal.

This is also true of physical pain. The suffering-self (actor) feels justified in taking the action of hurting. Once the wisdom of the mind rules over the testimony of our senses, even physical pain can be dissolved into a space-like vacuity and it will be gone too. That is, the knowledge of emptiness arises and the pain disappears into a space like vacuity.

Chapter 9

Fundamental Principals OF
The Middle Way
Commentary

An Examination
Of What Comes First?

In several chapters we have shown that cause and effect can't be established with the cause coming first. How can a cause be a cause if it's not causing anything. And the effect can't come first, because then we would have an effect without a cause. Yet this seems to be what happens.

Who comes first, the father or the son? If our existence was real, the father would have to come first. However, as mentioned before, a father can't be a father until after he has a son. So how can the father come first? So it seems the son comes first, but this is impossible too. How can a son be a son without a father? How can there be an effect without a cause? There is only one answer to this dilemma. Cause and affect has to be an illusion, like a magician's trick.

And for the past few chapters we have demonstrated that cause and affect can't be established based on actors and actions, perceivers and objects of perception, etc. Original text says that nothing really exists. The Buddha says, "All things in *samskara,* the seemingly real world, are like reflections of the moon in water, mirages, or bubbles which is without any substance whatsoever.

Even life force can't be found anywhere. And he comes to the final conclusion which might be misunderstood by all, "that nothing exists." For this reason Kenpho Tsultrim Gyamtso has written a wonderful small poem to counter all such misinterpretations.

"When you think, 'I exist,' or, 'I don't exist,'
That's how you fall into realism or become a nihilist.
To know the true nature, think of the clear sky at night.
And on a beautiful lake, a moon that shines so bright.
Appearance and emptiness that no one can separate –
That's how to meditate."

Chapter 10

Fundamental Principals OF
The Middle Way
Commentary

An Examination Of
Fire and Burning Wood.

Nagarjuna wrote this chapter on fire and burning wood because some people said, fire and burning wood are real, and they exist exactly like the self and the aggregates, which must be real too.

In order to refute this claim, Nagarjuna had to use logical arguments to prove that fire and burning wood are not real. And in the same way prove the self and the aggregates are not real too.

There were 5 things that Nagarjuna uses to prove the fire and burning-wood are unreal.

1, The burning-wood itself is not the fire.

2, There is no fire apart from the burning-wood

3, The fire does not possess the burning-wood.

4, The fire does not support the burning-wood,

5, and the burning-wood does not support the fire.

The first argument is true because the fire would be the actor and the burning-wood would be the action. Actors and actions require there to be duality. Therefore the burning-wood and the fire must be different.

The second argument is true because burning wood and fire can not exist separately. If they could, fire could exist in one place and the the burning-wood in another. Therefore, fire can't exist apart from the burning-wood.

The last three arguments are true also. In order for all three of these to be true, the supporter and support as well as the possessor and possesse have to each be the same thing. None of them can exist all alone – by themselves – separately.

The first (1st) argument proves the fire and the burning wood are not the same thing. But the second (2nd), third (3rd), fourth (4th), and fifth (5th) arguments prove the fire and the burning wood are the same thing. If fire and burning wood were real, they could not exist logically this way. Therefore, they would have to be an illusion because nothing can be the same and different at the same time.

Therefore fire and burning wood are not real – empty of inherent existence – appearance emptiness only.

The self and feelings (or the self and any of the 5 aggregates) would be exactly the same as the fire and firewood. Since we are concentrating of emotional pain, we shall chose the aggregate of feelings

1, The self and feelings (emotional pain) are not the same thing.

2, The self is not something different from feelings (emotional pain).

3, The self does not possess any feelings (emotional pain).

4, The self does not exist in dependence on feelings (emotional pain).

5, Feelings (emotional pain) do not exist in dependence of the self.

The first argument is true. This is because the self is the actor and emotional pain is the action. Logically action and the actor must be different.

The second argument is true also because the self and feelings do not appear apart from each other. This means they are one and the same thing.

The next three arguments are true also because they are not different things. Support and the supporter as well as the possessor and the possesse can't arise by themselves – all alone – individually. Where has there ever been a supporter without the thing being supported? When has there ever been a possessor without a possesse? Where has anyone been dependent without something to depend on. These arguments proves the self must be the same as feelings (emotional pain).

In the same way as fire and burning-wood are not real, the self and feelings are also not real – empty of inherent existence.

The first (1ˢᵗ) argument tells us feelings and the self are different.

The second (2ⁿᵈ), third (3ʳᵈ), fourth (4ᵗʰ), and fifth (5ᵗʰ) arguments tell us the opposite: that is, the self and feelings are exactly the same thing.

Noting real could exist this way. How can something be real and at the same time be both different and the same as itself?

Using the above logic, emotional pain will dissolve into a space-like vacuity and will be immediately gone. We have just inferentially realized the emptiness of the self: that is, unreal, like a dream self, and totally unreal. Therefore realizing the emptiness of the self is a very useful thing whenever there is any emotional or physical pain. That's because all pain can actually be pacified with this method in only a few days or weeks.

Disclaimer: In this Chapter Nagarjuna seems to contradict himself claiming in this chapter possessor and possesses are the same thing and in other chapters declaring them different. This is not a contradiction. It proves emptiness from a single perspective.

In Chapter 20, for example, Nagarjuna says possessors and possesses do exist conventionally, but they are empty because we can never find the possessor. For example in the *namarupa*, meditation: that is, Understanding Ontology Part 1, we could not find the forest, the trees or even our own body in the outside world.

The only thing we could find were the parts of the forest, trees and body. That's because the possessor of these parts is not to be found outside of the mind where we think they should be. Instead the forest, trees, etc are inside our own mind, making then unreal, like an illusion or like a dream.

Chapter 11

Fundamental Principals OF
The Middle Way
Commentary

An Examination of Samskara

Nagarjuna wrote this chapter because of people who said, the self is real because *samskara* is real. If *samskara* were unreal, there would NOT be anybody going around in it. And because the self goes around in it, the self must be real also. In the previous chapter Nagarjuna proved the self is unreal. In this chapter, he also proves s*amskara* unreal.

There Is No Perception Of A
Beginning, Middle and End
For Samskara To Exist Inherently

Based on cause and effect, there is no way *samskara* could have ever begun. Originally supposedly nothing existed. So how could two things have come together inherently to get it all started?

Chapter 1 proves nothing exists without causes and conditions. So whatever causes and conditions there were from beginningless time has led to our our present state of causes and conditions. However, no matter how hard we try, we can never find an original cause. And this would have been necessary to prove *samskara* began because of inherently real cause and effect.

Yes, causes and conditions do exists. But there is only an appearance – appearance emptiness – like in a dream. The causes do not really cause anything and the conditions do not exist inherently. So samskara is like an illusion and beginningless. Therefore, an inherently real middle can never begin. If a beginning and middle never began inherently, how can there be a real end?

If the self really went around in samskara, how did it all begin? Did the self come first or did *samskara* come first?

If the self came first, there would be nowhere for it to have existed.

If samskara came first, there would be no self to go around in it. This is due of the following facts.

There are 12 links in the chain of cause and affect that create *samskara*. These are called, "The twelve (12) Links of Dependent Arising." The first link is ignorance. The way it appears, for every act of ignorance, there is a corresponding and directly proportional reaction of karma that causes *duka* (Sanskrit) which means suffering.

In *Madhyamaka* good karma is suffering as well as bad karma, but as long as we are fooled by *samskara* into believing it is real, we do not consider good karma as something bad. However, good karma is just as bad as bad karma, because karma is the only thing causing our ignorance – the only thing causing suffering.

Samskara is all the aggregates:

> 1, Form
> 2, Feelings
> 3, Perceptions
> 4, Mental activity
> 5, Consciousness

It include everything perceived by the self. So if *samskara* came first, there would be no self to experience it. That is, the aggregates don't exist until there is a self to experience them. Is there revenge, for example, without a self to accomplished it? How can there be pain without someone to experience it?

Therefore, if *samskara* did come first, there would be no self to bring the aggregates into existence. If *samskara* came first, for example, this would represent our body coming first along with all the other aggregates. Each self, for example, has a unique and different body. So how could our body with the millions and perhaps billions of unique features ever come into being without a self to give it the individualism. This proves that when samskara and a self do combine to bring each other into existence, it can't be due to inherent cause and affect. Logically it can only be imputed – like a dream – unreal – appearance emptiness.

The point here is not that the self and *samskara* do or don't exist. The point is that it's illogical to believe they could ever come into existence due to inherently real cause and effect.

Samskara and the self can't come together simultaneously because they could not act as a cause for each other. In fact neither exists without the other. That means that neither can really exist independently, and therefore, they would never be able to act simultaneously or sequentially to create a cause and effect relationship.

Therefore, the self and samskara can not come together sequentially due to cause and effect or simultaneously. Yes they do come into existence but neither are actually real.

Additionally, ignorance can never be a cause until after there is an effect. In the case of a volatile substance and a spark, which comes first, the spark or the explosion? The spark can't come first. This is because the spark that caused the explosion can't be that spark until after the explosion takes place.

Which comes first, the father or the son? The father can't come first because a father can't be a father until after there is a son. In the same way, ignorance can't be the original cause to begin the 12 links until after *samskara* has already caused some karma. This is totally illogical which means the self, *samskara* and ignorance are all totally unreal.

Yes, they do come together but it is only an appearance – appearance emptiness – imputed like in a dream – all together. It appears to be cause and effect but it's like an illusion – not real.

In this chapter Nagarjuna also discusses birth and death. This only happens in s*amskara*. So if there is really no one to go around in it, how can *samskara* be real? Therefore, reincarnation and karma aren't real either. We are never really born, nor do we really die. So whatever we have heard about enlightenment taking many lifetimes, it might be worth re-examining.

The facts in this chapter points to a single fact: that is, the only thing holding us back from enlightenment is faith that it can happen now. If *samskara* and the self don't really exist, then who or what is blocking our path?

Is merit holding us back? No! Merit is not real either.

Is good karma holding us back? No! Good karma is not real either.

Is meditation holding us back? No! Meditation is not real either.

This leaves only one thing, faith! Most important!

Chapter 12

Fundamental Principals OF
The Middle Way
Commentary

An Examination
Of Suffering

Nagarjuna composed this chapter because of people who said that because suffering exists, the self that experiences it is also real.

This chapter deals with disconnecting the sense faculties from the objects of the senses. In Raja Yoga this is called *pratyahara* (Sanskrit) which involves mostly will power. This chapter deals with how to do it based only on logic and reason – an easier and softer way. Based on logic and reason, we realize that suffering is not real.

It's like the suffering happening in a fictitious stage play or a movie. How can the suffering take place? There's really no one on stage or in the movie who actually undergoes any physical events in the story. It's all make believe – an illusion – never really happens.

If we can disconnect the sense faculties from the self or object of our senses, then NO physical suffering and NO emotional suffering can take place. We might get upset and become angry, fearful or depressed – suffering terribly or becoming very happy during a movie. I actually remember having these kinds of experience when I first stated seeing movies at about six-years-of-age.

But as soon as we realize the movie isn't real, our suffering ends. This fact – that it's not real – automatically disconnects our senses from our self.

In the same way suffering in a nightmare ends as soon as we realize it's only a dream – NOT real! This, too, automatically disconnects our senses form self. And finally, in our supposedly real life our senses are automatically disconnected from our self once we realize that neither suffering nor our self is actually real.

There are many logical reasons why suffering is not real. Some of them have already been given. Here are a few of them.

In Chapter 10 we proved there is no one really there to actually suffer.

In the Chapter 2 we learned that coming and going is not real. Since suffering comes and goes, it is automatically unreal. It doesn't come from anywhere and doesn't go anywhere. It can't.

In another chapter we learned that suffering and the one who suffers (the self) are not the same thing. But there is no suffering apart form the one who suffers. Otherwise, the self could exist in one place and suffering could exist in another. This makes the self totally unreal. Noting can be the same and different from the self at the same time.

The causal conditions in Chapter 1 don't really exist. That means that neither the self nor suffering can arise in any of the four (4) extremes covered in Chapter 1. Therefore, neither the self nor suffering can arise due to inherent cause and affect. But it does arise as appearance only – appearance emptiness – like in a dream. Even though it appears like cause and effect, it's not.

All this means that we suffer because it's like we are dreaming. But we don't really know it. When wisdom arises that the self and suffering are NOT real, *samskara* dissolves into a space-like vacuity and all suffering – physical and emotional – end immediately. At the same time the knowledge of emptiness arises and pain disappears.

Nagarjuna has a beautiful verse 10 in his manuscript which is as follows:

That which is suffering does not arise
from any of the four (4) extremes, and not only that
All outer phenomena do NOT arise
From any of the four (4) extremes either.

Once we dissolve suffering into a space-like vacuity, the

self that exists with it, disappears. Only the observer remains. Hurray! We have just inferentially realized emptiness of the self on the second Mahayana Path. But even though it's inferential and not yet a direct realization, it will kill all emotional pain immediately and even some minor physical pain too.

Test Time

At this point when we hurt the next time, it might be a good idea to go back to the first chapter as a review of what we know. We can ask ourselves:

1, Did our pain arise of itself?
2, Did it arise by itself or by another?
3, By both itself and another?
4, Or did it arise because of causes and conditions?

There is no other possibility.

In order to pass the test, dissolve the pain into an inferential realization of emptiness. If so, congratulations you have just been promoted to the Second (2nd) Mahayana Path, the path of Superior Seeing.

The next step is a Direct experience of emptiness: that is, The Third (3rd) Path, The Path of Direct Seeing.

Chapter 13

Fundamental Principals OF
The Middle Way
Commentary

An Examination
Of The Precise Nature of Reality

This chapter is just a reminder that even though everything exists, it doesn't exist inherently. It exists only as something unreal. This has very much been repeated in all the chapters from the beginning, so it's a little redundant to mention it again. It's a reminder that Buddhas see the world of *samskara* as totally unreal. On the other hand we see the world as real and that's entirely why we suffer.

Chapter 14

Fundamental Principals OF
The Middle Way
Commentary

An Examination
Of Contact

Using another poem by Khenpo Tsultrim Gyamtso that really describes it beautifully:
"In this great expanse without center or end,
On this planet with neither top nor bottom,
Friends and enemies it seems,
Are forever meeting and parting,
But please know, it's all like a dream."

In order for contact to occur, it's necessary for the sense perception (lets assume a form), to make contact with the sense consciousness (the eye) which in turn is relayed to the self (seer). Then they would have to meet causing an inherent reaction either sequentially or simultaneously.

The sense perception (the form) can't come together in cause and effect with the eye. This is because neither can exist alone – all by itself – individually. How can there be a perception (the form) without a perceiver (the eye)? Yes, they come to together but not by cause and effect. They are imputed like in a dream. This means they can't inherently come together sequentially.

And they can't come together simultaneously because in

order to do that, they must both inherently exist individually first, which they don't. This means they can't really come together sequentially nor simultaneously. Neither can exist all by itself first to cause anything from the other.

The self (the perceiver) can't exist alone by itself either. If it did, it would be a seer with nothing seen. Ultimately this means that the sense perception (the form), the object of perception (the eye,) and the seer (the self) are all unreal. None of them can stand alone in a real inherently existence to ever be involved in real cause and effect. This is because they are not real themselves.

Therefore, in the meeting of these three (3) things, they can't meet as pairs nor can they meet all together.

Emotional Suffering
Also Involves Three Sets Of Pairs.
The Same As All The Aggregates

1, There is the sense object (emotional pain
      – lets assume depression)
2, There is the perceiver of sense objects (feelings)
3, And the self who experiences the pain.

None of the above three pairs can exist inherently all alone – by themselves – individually. Therefore based on common sense and reason, none of them can be involved in inherent cause and effect. Instead they all begin together as a unit when they are imputed – like and illusion – like in an unreal dream.

Therefore, their appearance as well as all emotional pain is all unreal appearance – appearance emptiness.

This means that all humans who think their contact is real suffer. The practice then is the scientifically letting go of all aspects of contact: that is, letting go of all pain and suffering – emotional as well as physical – realizing it isn't real. When this happens, the mind dissolves into a space-like vacuity and all emotional pain is gone immediately with an inferential realization of emptiness. At the same time the knowledge of emptiness arises and the pain disappears.

Chapter 15

Fundamental Principals OF
The Middle Way
Commentary

An Examination Of
Things And The Absence Of Things

Nagarjuna wrote this chapter for people who believed that things are real because causes and conditions exist to produce them. And these same people also believe that because there is a lack of causes and conditions, nothing really exists there. He wrote it for well meaning people who were trying to follow his instructions to realize emptiness but were confused.

Noting inherently real can exist in any of the four extremes discussed in Chapter 1. Yet things do exist as appearances only. Chapter 1 seems quite clear and we think we understand it. But many get trapped in the middle, so to speak.

Being trapped in the middle is getting trapped in existence and nonexistence. Since Ultimate Reality is non-conceptual and *samskara* is totally conceptual, there is no way to describe Ultimate Reality in conceptual words. The *Madhyamaka* view is that ultimate reality neither exists, nor does it not exist. Yes, *samskara* exists but it exists in a certain way. The way it exists is, it neither exists nor does it not exist. It exists somewhere between realism and nihilism. This is the non-conceptual way it exists.

Existence and nonexistence are concepts. They are a pair of opposites like hot and cold, high and low, black and white, etc. So those who are trapped in the middle think, since causes and conditions are there, something is there. But according to *Madhyamaka,* there is neither existence there, nor is there nonexistence there. That's the something that's there.

In the same way, the lack of causes and conditions might

lead one to think conceptually, there's nothing there. *Madhyamaka* view is, there is neither nothing there, nor is there something there. And this same thing is true with all the pairs of conceptual opposites. Things are neither hot nor cold, they are neither cold nor are they hot. That's the something that's there Ultimately.

There is no emotional pain there but at the same time it is not absent of emotional pain. This sounds ridiculous of course. But something non-conceptual can't be expressed in words which are themselves conceptual. Brahman nor Emptiness can be described in words. That's one of the reasons why.

When our six (6) sense faculties detect the aggregates, this happens non-conceptually. So when *Madhyamaka* refers to existence, it's this non-conceptual existence to which it refers. The self, however, conceptualizes everything.

Everything conceptualized is unreal. It's appearance only – appearance emptiness!

Once the self perceives the aggregates, they get conceptualized. Only then are things hot or cold, existing or non existing, etc. Once we get a direct experience of emptiness, then we will have this non-conceptual view. The trick is to scientifically let go of the self: that is, realize the emptiness of the self. Then we will be free of all suffering. If there is no ego self, there is no existence and no nonexistence – no conceptual fabrications.

Realizing the emptiness of the self is the true refuge from all pain and suffering. There is no other refuge so sublime and protective. The Hindus call it the realization of Brahman, the true self. In Sanskrit, the Hindus say there are two selves, *ahamkara* the ego or false self and the *autman* or Real Self.

The Buddhists say there is only one self, the false self, *ahamkara* or ego. Realizing the emptiness (or unreality) of this self kills all emotional pain. But this false self still exists like everything else in *samskara*. But how does it exist? The answer is, non conceptually – somewhere between existence and non existence. Many Hindus call it a selfless self.

This seems like two different philosophies – one Buddhist and one Hindu. But are they different? Both are monists. The Buddhists claim only emptiness really exists. Hindus claim only Brahman really exists. Other than how it's explained, where's the difference?

In order to clarify Chapter 1, Nagarjuna wrote the following verse:

"Existence is the view of permanence,
   Nonexistence is the view of extinction,
   Therefore, the wise do not get trapped
   In existence or nonexistence."

Existence and nonexistence both require the false self or ego to understand what is meant: that is, conceptualize them.

Here is one of the easiest ways to realize the emptiness of the self. Think of anything and the try to imagine it as neither existing or non-existing at the same time. Concentrate on each concept alternately. What's in between is revealed when the ego lets go. Once the self lets go, there is an inferential realization of the emptiness of self. At the same time, it's totally possible to get a glimpse of what non-conceptual means. At the very same time the knowledge of emptiness of the self arises and all conceptual fabrication ceases. The Hindus call it the realization of Brahman.

And by the way, if there was any emotional pain happening, it will be gone also. And this happens long before emptiness or Brahman is realized directly. How long will it take? Not more than a few days or weeks.

Chapter 16

Fundamental Principals OF
The Middle Way
Commentary

An Examination
Of Bondage & Liberation

The scriptures state that bondage and liberation are unreal so, therefore, nothing is bound and, therefore, nothing needs any liberation. Nagarjuna wrote this chapter for those who doubted these scriptures.

Jay Mipham's commentary analyzes the aggregates. If the aggregates were real and wandering in samskara, they would have to either be permanent or temporary. There is no third alternative.

If the aggregates were real and permanent they could not wander at all. Real permanence means nothing can change. Their position can't change, so they can't wander.

And if the aggregates were real and temporary they could also not wander at all. As soon as the aggregates arose, since they are temporary, they would have to disappear. And the same is true of human beings. Therefore, neither the aggregates nor sentient beings can wander in *samskara*. Therefore, samskara must be like an illusion, unreal – with nobody really wandering in it.

Beyond that Chapter 11 also provides sound reasoning why sentient beings don't wander in *samskara,* so nobody is bound and nobody needs liberation. Therefore, know for sure that enlightenment can happen right now. If we were bound, it might take many, many years, lifetimes or ages. But since we ware not bound, have faith and it can happen immediately.

Chapter 17

Fundamental Principals OF
The Middle Way
Commentary

An Examination
Of Karmic Actions
And Results

Nagarjuna wrote this chapter for people who thought karma was holding back his or her enlightenment. If karmic actions and results did not exist, then it would be impossible for *samskara* to exist as well. This is absolutely true since Chapter 8 tells us no karmic actions take place because there's no self (actor) to make karmic actions and results. And there could be no karmic results happening because there is no self that could be directly affected by them.

Other chapters tell us the same thing. Anything more seems redundant.

Chapter 18

Fundamental Principals OF
The Middle Way
Commentary

An Examination of
Self & Phenomena

This is a very important chapter. The emptiness of self and phenomena many claim to be the most important teaching of the Buddha. The emptiness of self has already been explained in Chapter 10, Fire and Burning Wood, which discusses five (5) key points. In this chapter Nagarjuna covers only one (1). That is, are the aggregates the same or different than the self?

The five aggregates: 1, Form - 2, Feelings - 3, Perceptions - 4, Mental activity - 5, Consciousness.

The aggregates include everything in *samskara* that can be experienced by the self. Long commentary on this chapter may be redundant too. But I'm still going to do it because of the importance of this chapter.

If the aggregates were the same as the self, it would arise and cease along with the aggregates. How many selves are there? Only one? If the self were the same as feelings, there would be an infinite number of selves. This is because every day there is an infinite number of feelings that happen.

And if the self were the same as each of those feelings, there would be just as many selves. Additionally if the self was the same as the body, the self would change moment by moment as the body changes. Or with every change of the body, the self would die and be reborn new – moment by moment. Additionally each part of the body would command a different self: that is, the self of the hand, foot, stomach, etc.

Finally if the self and the aggregates were the same, the self could not possess them. We could no longer say, my head, my hand, my feelings, my money, etc. This is because for the self to possess anything, the self must be different from the aggregate it possesses. Obviously if the self were the same as the aggregates, it would not be separate and could not do this.

However, the self can not be different from the aggregates either. This is because if the self were real and different from the aggregates it could not change. Therefore, it could not do any of the things it normally did. It couldn't die and be reborn.

All of the functions the self can perform are included in the aggregates. If it did not have any of these characteristics, it could not do anything. It couldn't have feelings. It couldn't have the six (6) sense bases. It would be inert and unable to do anything.

Since we can't be the same and different than the aggregates, that means the self and aggregates are unreal. Therefore, both the self and aggregates must be like an illusion, unreal, like a dream self – appearance emptiness.

Based on this simple reasoning, it's not necessary to have all the arguments in Fundamental Principals. These simple arguments in Chapter 18 are all that's necessary. That's because logically it proves the self and the aggregates (everything in *samskara*) to be nothing more than appearance emptiness.

Nagarjuna stresses that we only need renounce the aspects of me and mine. In this case no self will be experienced. No emotional pain will be experienced and no physical pain will be experienced as well. This is a great way to kill emotional pain in meditation. But from the author's personal experience this is not easy to do at work. In fact it seemed impossible.

One of Nagarjuna's verses reads:
If there's no, "Me," in the first place,
How could there be anything that belongs to me,
When, "Me," and, "Mine," are peace,

Clinging to, "Me," and, "Mine," ceases.

Dissolving any emotional pain into an inferential realization of emptiness using any logical facts is a unique experience. The emotional pain turns to infallible peace as the mind moves into a space-like vacuity.

The way to analyze this chapter is to wait until there is some emotional or physical pain. Then ask ourselves, are we the same as the aggregates? The same as the anger, fear, depression or guilt, etc? If we were the same as the aggregates, for example anger, and if the self were real, no change would be possible. So if we were angry, it would mean we have always been angry.

And since we can remember what caused the anger this time, this is not the case. NO, we have not always been angry.

Then we can ask ourselves, are we different from the anger? If we were different from the anger and it were real, no change is possible. It would be impossible to be angry. Or if angry, it would mean we were always angry.

Hey wait a minute! How can this be? We must be the same or different than our anger. There is no third choice. Our anger can't exist like that, but it does? Therefore, it must be like an illusion or like dream anger. The anger can't be real. And the self that experiences the anger can't be real either. They are appearance only! Appearance emptiness!

By looking at the anger and rehashing this logic over and over, the anger disappears into a space-like vacuity. And even if the logic is not understood, by taking it on BLIND FAITH the anger isn't real, it will still dissolve into a space-like vacuity. Eventually the self will finally let go of it's conceptual hold on the ill will. Then the details of what happened: that is, who did what and to whom can be analyzed non-conceptually – without the self seeking revenge.

One of the biggest problems of letting go for the author was the possibilities of loop-holes. I kept trying to figure out how something real might also be able to change. I kept holding onto the self despite all the logic against it. Simply, something real can"t change.

I kept thinking about gold which changes very little over time. But it's atomic structure can be changed with modern science. In that case nothing is real, I thought. Finally I just gave up and accepted the arguments on blind faith. We are the ones that have to give up, throw in the towel so to speak. And when I did, my anger dissolved into nothing. It still arises but it can be pacified this way easily.

There's more to discussed in Chapter 18, but it's beyond the scope of killing emotional and physical pain.

Chapter 19

Fundamental Principals OF
The Middle Way
Commentary

An Examination
of Time

Covered in Ontology 2

Chapter 20

Fundamental Principals OF
The Middle Way
Commentary

An Examination
Of Collections

Collections of things are things like schools of fish, forests, armies, head of hair – all the plurals. This is what the Hindus call the *nama rupa* meditation covered in Ontology 1. Everything is plural, it's name and it's parts. What about the elements? Gold for example that has no parts. Gold as well as everything else has parts if we consider the inside and outside, right side, left side, etc. And finally gold would be a plural simply from having an identifying characteristic as all elements – covered in Chapter 5. We find the parts in the outside world, but we can't find the possessor of the parts where they are supposed to be – outside in the seemingly real world. Instead we find the possessor only exists in our own mind. .

Therefore, all of the aggregates are appearance emptiness, unreal, like things in a dream.

Chapter 21

Fundamental Principals OF
The Middle Way
Commentary

An Examination Of
Emergence & Decay

Nagarjuna wrote this chapter because of people who believed hat time produced emergence and decay. For example, a person is born, and over time, grows old, and dies. The grass is green in the summer and brown in the winter and again green in the summer. Since all this happens over time, emergence, decay and time must, therefore, be real.

This is analyzed by inquiry into whether emergence and decay are the same thing or are they different things? They are not the same thing, They are conceptual opposites, like hot and cold, light and dark, existence and nonexistence, etc. Therefore they can not be the same.

But at the same time, they can not be different things totally independent from each other. This is because each depends on it's existence from the other. Emergence of a flower depends on the flower for it's emergence and it also depends on the flower for it's decay. In this case emergence is necessary for decay to happen. Therefore, they can't be different.

This is exactly the same case as Chapter 10, Fire and Firewood. Only in this case we have emergence and decay. Fire and firewood depend on each other for their existence in the same way emergence and decay depend on each other for their existence.

A thing is either the same or different. There's no third choice. The trick in realizing emptiness is to force the logic of our intellect to rule over the testimony of our senses. Yes, greed, anger, fear, depression and guilt emerge and decay. They arise (emerge) and (decay) die out (become less in time and eventually cease).

Is the emergence of the emotional pain different or the same thing as the dying out? Of course they're different!

But are they really different? The dying out or the decay of the emotional pain depends entirely on the very fact that it arose in the first place. So how can it be different?

Apart form the emergence of emotional pain there is no decay (dying off) possible. And since there is no third choice, therefore, the emergence of emotional pain and it's decay is like an illusion, unreal, appearance emptiness. Nothing can be the same and different from itself at the same time.

The trick here is to realize that good (happiness) and bad (emotional pain) are different using the testimony of our senses to conceptualize our argument. Consequently we suffer.

But at the same time we can use the testimony of our intellect to conceptualize they are NOT different. Consequently we can end our suffering. This is done, for example, by realizing intellectually that greed, anger, fear, depression or guilt is the same as any kind of happiness.

When this happens, we have two (2) opposing conceptual ideas. Only an illusion can exist like this. So the self eventually lets go of the conceptualization of these senses and it's seen for what it really is, appearance emptiness.

The real thick is to let go of both the intellectual concept and the testimony of our senses concept. In order to realize emptiness we must go beyond all concepts. Emptiness, Brahman, Divine Mind, etc. are non-conceptual.

And when the observer backs away form both of these concepts we realize the emptiness of self which is infallible bliss and peace. Remember always, emptiness is beyond all conceptual fabrications.

Chapters 22

Has nothing to do with emotional Pain so it's omitted.

Chapter 23

Has little to do with emotional Pain so it's omitted also.

Chapter 24

Little to do with emotional pain so omitted also.

Chapter 25

Fundamental Principals OF
The Middle Way
Commentary

An Examination Of
Samskara & Nirvana

There are only two important verses I believe as far as ending emotional pain is concerned.

In the 19th Verse Nagarjuna says,

> Samskara is not the least bit different
> > from Nirvana.
> Nirvana is not the slightest bit different
> > than Samskara.

The 20th Verse reads,

> The true nature of Nirvana
> > is the true nature of Samskara.
> The true nature of Samskara
> > is the true nature of Nirvana.

So everything exists in samskara and Nirvana. This means that enlightenment is not something other than what we experience in samskara. The real question then, is the enlightened being still subject to the laws of karma – laws of causation? Here is a Zen story that explains it vividly.

Hyakujo's Fox

Once when Hyakujo delivered some Zen lectures an old man attended them, unseen by the monks. At the end of each talk when the monks left so did he. But one day he remained after they had gone, and Hyakujo asked him: "Who are you?"

The old man replied: "I am not a human being, but I was a human being when the Kashapa Buddha preached in this world. I was a Zen master and lived on this mountain. At that time one of my students asked me whether the enlightened man is subject to the law of causation. I answered him: The enlightened man is not subject to the law of causation."

"For this answer evidencing a clinging to *absoluteness* I became a fox for five hundred rebirths, and I am still a fox. Will you save me from this condition with your Zen words and let me get out of a fox's body? Now may I ask you: Is the enlightened man subject to the law of causation?"

Hyakujo said: "The enlightened man is one with the law of causation."

At the words of Hyakujo the old man was enlightened. "I am emancipated," he said, paying homage with a deep bow. "I am no more a fox, but I have to leave my body in my dwelling place behind this mountain. Please perform my funeral as a monk." Then he disappeared.

The next day Hyakujo gave an order through the chief monk to prepare to attend the funeral of a monk. "No one was sick in the infirmary," wondered the monks. "What does our teacher mean?"

After dinner Hyakujo led the monks out and around the mountain. In a cave, with his staff he poked out the corpse of an old fox and then performed the ceremony of cremation.

That evening Hyakujo gave a talk to the monks and told this story about the law of causation.

Therefore, even though there is nothing different between Nirvana and samskara, the enlightened being is one with everything. And consequently can never be affected with suffering again. It takes two things for suffering to take place. There must be feelings of hurt and a self to experience that hurt.

If the enlightened being becomes one with the laws of samskara, there is no longer two. Can fire burn itself? Neither can an enlightened being be burned.

The reason Samskara and Nirvana are exactly the same is because they are logically the same thing (Chapter 10 and Chapter 21). Yes, conceptually they are opposites. But at the same time they are conceptually the same thing. If Nirvana were real and one gained it by acquiring wisdom, which comes first the ignorance or the or the wisdom? Neither can exist on their own. Like all concepts, neither can exist without the other. They depend on each other. So neither can come first. That means that they can't come together by cause and effect sequentially or simultaneously. Therefore, they can't be inherently real.

How they actually exist is by being imputed instantly as a single entity – together on the mind conceptually.

Another reason why they are the same thing is for the same reason as emergence and decay are the same (Chapters 10 & 21). Yes, they too are conceptual opposites. But at the same time they are the same thing because they depend on each for their existence.

In the same way depression is the same thing as gratitude. Yes, they too are conceptual opposites. But at the same time they are are the same thing because neither can come first. Also a second reason is both depend on each other.

So the very next time we're depressed, realize that depression is the same thing as dignity, honor and peace of mind. Yes, they are conceptual opposites! But logically they are also conceptually the same thing. Nothing real can exist like this.

So Nirvana is the conceptual opposite of Samskara. Therefore they are both the same and opposite of each other based on two (2) different conceptions. But enlightenment is a non-conceptual realization. When the observer backs away from both concepts, bliss and infallible peace arise.

According to Nagarjuna and *Madhyamaka,* even this non-conceptual realization is not real. That's because it depends on wisdom. And we have already proven in all of the chapters of Fundamental Principals that anything dependent on anything else, for it's arising is – dependent arising – which by definition is unreal – appearance emptiness. .

Therefore when Ultimate Wisdom arises, we are permanently liberated form the conceptual aspect of *Samskara* and the conceptual aspect of Nirvana. And even though it's an experience of Ecstatic Bliss, of which a thousand bottles of whiskey can't compare, it too is also unreal. That is, emptiness is also empty. Enlightenment too is unreal.

Just in case this last chapter is a wrong view with some hidden **absoluteness**, like the teaching given by the zen master in Hyajujo's story, please pray for the author, so he will not have to spend the next 500 births in the body of a fox. Thanks...

Chapters 26 – 27
Little to do with emotional pain so omitted

www.ingramcontent.com/pod-product-compliance
Lightning Source LLC
Chambersburg PA
CBHW050919260726
48660CB00001B/298